FINANCIAL LITERACY ESSENTIALS

A Dollars and Sense Guide
For Young Adults

FINANCIAL
LITERACY
ESSENTIALS

BONUS FINANCIAL SUCCESS STARTER PACK!

As a thank you for your purchase, go to page 223 to find out how you can get a FREE BONUS Financial Success Starter Pack – a powerful PDF collection of insightful blog articles and infographics to help you take your financial journey to the next level!

TABLE OF CONTENTS

INTRODUCTION

FINANCIAL LITERACY FOR HIGH SCHOOL STUDENTS AND YOUNG ADULTS

So you're at the edge of a new chapter in life – whether it's graduating, preparing for that first job, or just stepping out into young adulthood. It's exciting, right? But with that excitement might come a little nagging worry about what's next – especially when it comes to your future…and money! Money plays a major role in our lives. It's not just something we use to make purchases or transfer digitally; it's something we often think about, stress over, and plan our whole lives around. The adult world of bills, bank accounts, and budgeting is waiting for you, and it all seems like a puzzle with too many pieces. You might wonder if you're ready for these new responsibilities. Guess what? You're not alone. Most young people feel exactly the same way. Navigating finances as a young adult can feel like trying to solve a Rubik's cube blindfolded.

The problem? A lack of financial education. It's complicated, and sometimes it feels unfair that you're thrown into adulthood without a clear guide on how to manage money. Schools often skip over practical life skills. Maybe you've had a brief lecture buried somewhere during a random special assembly, but that's not enough. That's why so many recent grads find themselves buried in student loan debt or struggling to save beyond their next paycheck. It's not your fault - it's a system that hasn't given young people the tools they need to succeed.

Julia was a stellar student who graduated from college with honors. She moved out from her parents' home, eager to start her adult life, only to end up overwhelmed by credit card debt. Within months of moving out, she racked up thousands of dollars of debt and was under a mountain so deep that she had to say goodbye to her independence and move back in with her parents. Julia underestimated the impact of interest rates and never kept track of her expenses. This scenario is real and happens often.

Studies show that one in five U.S. teenagers lacks basic financial literacy. Many struggle with simple things like budgeting, managing credit cards and loans, or even opening a bank account, which leads to costly mistakes. And these mistakes can seriously add up. Researchers from the National Financial Educators Council found that the average American loses about $1,389 each year just because they don't have the right financial knowledge. Wouldn't you rather have that $1,389 back in your pocket?

Why is financial education so important? Well, the answer is very simple: by knowing the basics, you can shape a secure financial future for yourself.

Throughout this book, we'll look at the various pitfalls of financial illiteracy—like falling into debt, stressing over money, and becoming a victim of identity theft—and you'll see how proper education can help you avoid these traps. Learning financial literacy is like learning a new language—but it's a language that helps you navigate the adult world with ease. Being financially literate means understanding how to manage money, create budgets, and even invest wisely. By the end of this book, you'll have the knowledge to navigate the complex financial landscape ahead confidently.

No one is born with the ability to manage personal finances; it's a skill that must be learned. Yet, our current education system often neglects practical financial education, leaving students unprepared for real-world responsibilities. Just like math, financial literacy should be taught progressively, starting with the basics in elementary school and building on that foundation through middle and high school, and even into college. The curriculum should cover age-appropriate topics such as the value of money, saving, investing, and spending wisely. By the time students graduate, they should not only have a firm grasp of academic subjects but also a solid understanding of personal finance—skills they will use every day.

Financial literacy should be like any other subject we learn in school. Just like we're taught math to solve equations or history to understand our past, teaching us how to manage money effectively can equip us to navigate our financial futures. It's not just about balancing a checkbook—though even that seems foreign to many young people today—but understanding budgeting, saving, credit scores and investing, and then using that basic knowledge to make smart financial decisions.

So here's the good news: This book is crafted with your concerns in mind. You'll find relatable examples, practical advice, and interactive exercises designed to teach you the essentials, giving you confidence and helping you build solid financial habits.

Why should you listen to us? Well, we're a group of professionals from varied backgrounds in finance—banking, investing, tax planning, and insurance. Personal financial management has been a passion of ours for as long as any of us can remember. We've spent years diving deep into financial literacy, gaining credentials along the way, speaking and teaching on some of the topics you'll read about here in this book and working with both individuals and businesses to explain the basics and improve financial outcomes.

Think of us as your trusted guides; we've come together and made it our mission to cut through the noise and give you straightforward advice backed by solid evidence. Each of us recognized early on in our careers that high school, and sometimes even college, doesn't really prepare you for this stuff.

One common concern among young adults when it comes to financial literacy is the intimidating nature of financial terminology. Phrases like "interest rates," "stock market," "credit score" and "retirement accounts" can seem overwhelming. Throughout this book, we will break down these concepts into manageable chunks and in easy-to-understand language.

Another thing we often hear from young people like you is the fear of making financial mistakes—mistakes that could even stick with you for years. Is it smart to splurge on something today and then have no money left to fill up your gas tank tomorrow. Getting a credit card sounds cool and pretty straightforward, right? Swipe now, pay later. But, without understanding interest rates and the dangers of minimum payments, you could rack up a mountain of debt before you even realize what hit you. Then there's student loans. These can be a lifesaver in terms of paying for college, but they can also be a lifelong burden if you don't understand how repayment plans work or what kind of salary you can expect with your chosen career path. Research indicates that a lot of young people make uninformed decisions about taking out college loans, and these decisions have long-term sometimes negative consequences.

Our goal is to walk you through this knowledge step by step, so you can confidently manage your money and sidestep those financial landmines. We'll demystify financial concepts and provide you with practical tools to help you reach those dreams without feeling bogged down by jargon or complexity.

We'll explain the basics of financial literacy. We'll show you how to budget, save, spend and invest wisely. We'll delve into understanding credit scores, a concept that confuses many adults. You may not know this yet, but your credit score affects everything from your ability to rent an apartment, to the interest rate on your first car loan, even to the cost of covering that car with insurance. We'll demystify this by showing how different actions—like paying your bills on time, paying off a credit card early, or even just checking your credit report—can boost your credit score.

We'll tie it all together and show you how understating some basics of money management can help you be a smarter consumer, avoid the dangers of identity theft, and yes, even travel the world on a budget. You'll learn how your financial situation is affected not only by your decisions but also by basic economic principles and the world economy as a whole.

Finally, we'll look at how understanding your money mindset can help you make more thoughtful financial choices. You'll see how your emotional state can significantly impact your financial decisions and just by being mindful of that, it can keep you from making rash decisions that could harm your financial future.

Now, being financially literate isn't just about avoiding mistakes; it's also about seizing opportunities. Whether it's investing to grow your wealth or simply having the confidence to negotiate your first salary, solid financial knowledge opens doors.

Simply put, as with anything, the more confidence you have in your knowledge on any given topic, the better decisions you will make. Wouldn't you like to feel confident in your ability to manage money, make smart investments, and thereby, set yourself up for a prosperous future? With the knowledge you'll get from this book, you can begin the journey of a future where you are in control of your money, and not the other way around.

CHAPTER 1

UNDERSTANDING THE BASICS OF FINANCIAL LITERACY

Do you just walk into a store with no idea how much money you have in your pocket? Do you pick something off the shelf, head to the register, and hope for the best that you have enough to pay for it? Of course not! Now imagine living like that with your money every day – getting a paycheck and paying bills without keeping track. That's what financial *illiteracy* feels like, and unfortunately, it's a reality for many people. But here's the good news: the simple solution is money management and getting savvy with money management isn't as complicated as it sounds.

Think about all the times you've wanted to buy something but had to check your wallet first. If you've ever skipped out on plans because you were broke, or felt anxious seeing your friends spending freely while you held back, you already know why managing money matters.

This book simplifies the fundamental principles of financial literacy, made for high school students and young adults. We'll start with the basics of budgeting, showing you how to track income and expenses so you won't be left short at the end of the month. Then, we'll move on to saving strategies to help you build a safety net, from opening a savings account to setting up automatic deposits. Finally, we'll venture into the world of investing, breaking down terms like stocks and bonds and explain why starting early can make a big difference. We'll also cover borrowing responsibly, understanding debt, and protecting your assets with insurance. By the end of the book, you'll know how to set clear financial goals that align with your dreams and ambitions. Ready to unlock your financial superpowers? Let's get started!

The Basics of Financial Literacy

The term 'financial literacy' might sound a bit intimidating, but it's really just about understanding how to handle money smartly. This skill can help you plan your future, avoid stress, and achieve those big dreams. We'll delve deeper into some of the specifics, but here's a quick introductory overview of some key points.

Let's start with budgeting. Here's a scenario: You're going to the movies with friends. After buying your ticket, you have $20 left. Do you spend it all on a super-sized popcorn, candy, and a large soda or do you settle for a small snack and save the rest of the money for another day. Maybe you decide to skip the snack altogether. That is budgeting.

Creating a budget simply means deciding where your money goes before you spend it. The goal is to have more money coming in than going out so you need to set controls on when money goes out. Here's a quick guide on how to get started:

- First, set your financial goals: Think about what you want your money to do for you. Is it saving up for a new car or putting aside cash for college?
- Next, understand your income: This includes your allowance, part-time job earnings, or any other money you regularly receive.
- Then, track your spending: Write down where your money goes every week. Every single dollar. This might be your phone bill, snacks, or gas money.
- Finally, create your budget: Prioritize your essential "needs" over simple "wants" and ensure your expenses don't exceed your income.

One effective way to track this is by using a simple app or even a pen and paper. It might seem boring, but keeping track of where your money comes from and goes can really make a difference.

Moving on to saving - think of it as a contingency plan, a plan B in case plan A doesn't work. It's about setting aside money for future needs or emergencies. Imagine having enough saved up to cover unexpected expenses, like your laptop breaking right before finals—wouldn't that be a relief?

Here's how you can start saving:

- Open a savings account: Having a dedicated space for your savings helps keep it separate from daily spending monies. You can open one at a physical bank branch or online. Do some research and look for one that doesn't charge any fees or require you keep any minimum balance.
- Make regular deposits: Whether it's weekly, monthly, or whenever you get paid, consistency is key. You'll be surprised how even small amounts add up over time.
- Automate your savings: Set it up so a portion of your income goes directly into savings. Out of sight, out of mind!

Remember, saving isn't just about stashing away cash for a specific goal. It's also about building an emergency fund—enough to cover unexpected expenses. Only tap into this fund for genuine emergencies.

Next up, investing. It might sound complex, but let's break it down. Investing is about making your money work for you. Think of it like planting a tree; with the right care and time, it grows and bears fruit. When you invest, you're essentially buying assets like stocks, bonds, or mutual funds that can grow in value over time. And, investing early gives your investments more time to grow.

Getting started with investing requires some planning

- Determine your investment goals: Are you saving for college, a car, or just trying to build wealth for the future?
- Be consistent: Even if you're investing a small amount every week or month, stick to it and you'll be surprised how it adds up!

- Contribute to employer-sponsored plans: If your employer offers a retirement plan, it doesn't matter how old you are, if you are eligible - enroll in it and start saving! Especially if your employer matches your contributions, essentially this is them giving you money for free.

- Understand your risk tolerance: Every investment comes with risks, and it's important to balance these against your financial goals. Stocks tend to be riskier than bonds and even mutual funds differ between each other.

- Consider speaking with a financial advisor: They can offer guidance tailored to your needs. You don't have to go it alone. Some banks and financial institutions offer free advice, especially for new investors.

Let's talk about borrowing and debt management. Borrowing money isn't bad; but you need to be strategic and not borrow more than you can afford to pay back. For example, student loans can be a great investment in your future if managed wisely. However, runaway debt can lead to stress and financial troubles.

To borrow responsibly:

- Understand loan terms fully: Know the interest rate, repayment schedule, and total cost.

- Have a repayment plan: Decide how much you'll pay back monthly and stick to it.

- Avoid unnecessary debt: Only borrow what you can afford to repay without burdening yourself.

Protecting your assets is another critical aspect. This means safeguarding your savings, investments, and overall financial health.

- Build an emergency fund to cover the curveballs life throws at you.
- Get insurance to protect against major risks like health issues, accidents, or damage to property.

Financial literacy also includes understanding credit and credit scores. Your credit score is like a report card for how well you manage borrowed money. A good score can help you get better interest rates on loans and credit cards.

Maintaining a healthy credit score involves:

- Paying your bills on time: Timely payments boost your score.
- Keeping your credit utilization low: This means not maxing out your credit cards.
- Regularly checking your credit report for errors: Mistakes can happen, and catching them early helps maintain your score.

All of this comes together and helps you set realistic financial goals. Think of financial goals as a roadmap guiding you toward your dreams, whether that's owning a car, graduating college debt-free, or traveling the world.

Here's how to set effective financial goals:

- Differentiate between short-term and long-term goals: Short-term goals are ones you want to reach within a year, and long-term goals will require more than a year.
- Break down goals into manageable steps: Are you saving for a car? Then figure out what you can afford, the cost,

the insurance premiums and then you'll know how much you need to save each month.

- Use tools to track your progress: There are so many good apps out there but even simple spreadsheets or pen and paper can help.

- Regularly reassess and adjust your goals: Check your progress every now and then. Celebrate milestones, no matter how small, to stay motivated.

Understanding these principles equips you with the tools to make smart financial decisions. Financial literacy isn't something you master overnight; it's a continuous journey of learning and applying knowledge.

In conclusion, these skills - mastering budgeting, saving, investing, borrowing responsibly, protecting your assets, maintaining a good credit score, and setting clear financial goals - are the basics of financial literacy. Embrace them now, and you'll pave the way for a financially secure and fulfilling future. Start small, stay consistent, and watch how your financial landscape transforms over time.

Key Financial Terms Defined

When it comes to understanding how to manage money, the best place to start is by getting a good grasp on three key concepts: budgeting, saving, and investing. Think of these as your financial GPS—it helps you navigate where your money is going, guides you to save for emergencies or future goals, and shows you how to make your money grow over time.

Budgeting: Budgeting might seem like a boring task, but it's actually quite empowering once you get the hang of it. Essentially, a budget is a plan that outlines your income and expenses. By figuring out where your money is coming from and where it's going, you can make informed decisions about how to spend it or save it. Take a set amount of money each month and strike a balance between spending on essentials like food and rent and splurging on things you enjoy, like eating out with friends or a new outfit.

Here's what you can do to get started:

- Identify your net monthly income: This is the money you receive after taxes. Include all sources of income.
- List your monthly expenses: Consider both fixed expenses (the ones that are a set amount no matter what, like rent or car insurance) and variable ones (the ones you control, like clothing and entertainment).
- Subtract expenses from income: The difference will show if you have money left over or if you're overspending.
- Adjust as needed: If you find yourself short month after month, look for areas to cut back or ways to earn more.

And yes, it's as simple as that!

Budgeting isn't just about cutting back—it's about making conscious choices that reflect your priorities and goals. If you want to save up for a trip, buy a new gadget, or simply have a cushion for unexpected expenses, you have to plan ahead.

Saving: This is another crucial piece of the puzzle. Saving money isn't just for grown-ups, it's smart at any age, especially for those "just-in-case" moments. Emergencies happen—a surprise car repair, an unplanned expense, you name it. Having savings stashed away can really save the day.

Here are some tips to help you along:

- Start small: Even if it's just $10 a month, every bit adds up.
- Consider it as paying yourself first: Treat savings like a bill that must be paid.
- Create a separate savings account: This way, you'll be less tempted to dip into your savings for non-emergencies.
- Set clear goals: Know why you're saving. Whether it's for college, a new laptop, or simply for peace of mind, having a goal makes it easier to stay disciplined.

Once you've got the hang of budgeting and saving, you'll be ready to dive into investing.

Investing: This means putting your money into assets with the expectation that they will grow in value over time. This could be stocks, bonds, mutual funds, or even real estate. The cool thing about investing is that it allows your money to work for you.

To get started with investing:

- Learn the basics: Understand different types of investments and how they work.
- Start early: The earlier you start investing, the more time your money has to grow through compound interest.
- Diversify: Don't put all your money in one place. Spread it across various investments to reduce risk.

- Be patient: Investments can go up and down in value. Think long-term and don't panic during market fluctuations.

To wrap things up, remember that mastering budgeting, saving, and investing early on sets a solid foundation for your financial future. Sure, it might sound a bit overwhelming at first, but take it step-by-step. Start with tracking your income and expenses, then move on to saving regularly, and finally explore basic investing principles.

By getting a handle on these concepts now, you'll not only gain valuable skills but also set yourself up for greater financial freedom and security down the road. And hey, it's never too early to start thinking about your financial future. So, give it a go, experiment, and find what works best for you!

Summary

Laying the Foundation for Financial Success

Alright, let's wrap things up and bring this chapter home. We've journeyed through the essentials of financial literacy together, touching on everything from budgeting to investing, and borrowing responsibly to protecting your assets. These skills might seem overwhelming at first glance, but remember, each one is like a piece in the puzzle of securing your financial future.

Think back to our initial example: walking into the movie theater with $20 and deciding whether to splurge or save some for later. That simple decision mirrors the bigger choices you'll face as you navigate life. Budgeting, saving, investing, and managing debt all boil down to making smart choices about where your money goes.

Right now, you might be wondering why all this matters to you while you're still young. Well, imagine graduating without debt hanging over your head or having enough saved up to travel or start a business right after college. That's the kind of freedom solid money management can provide. It allows you to focus on your passions and ambitions without being held back by financial worries.

But here's the kicker—these skills aren't just about personal gain. They also equip you to make informed decisions that can benefit your community and society at large. Financially literate individuals can support local businesses, contribute to the economy, and even engage in philanthropy by giving to charities and causes you care about. On a broader scale, widespread financial literacy can lead to a more stable and fairer economic environment for everyone.

Financial literacy isn't something you master overnight; it's a continuous journey. Stay consistent, start small, and adapt as you go. The knowledge you're building now will serve you well throughout your life, helping you to not only achieve your dreams but also to weather any financial storms that come your way.

CHAPTER 2

EXPLORING PART-TIME JOBS AND ENTREPRENEURSHIP

Have you ever thought about what it feels like to earn your own money? Picture the excitement of holding your first paycheck in your hand, and knowing it's all from your hard work. Maybe you've scribbled down business ideas in a notebook or dreamed about being your own boss one day. Whether it's landing a part-time job at the local bakery or starting a small online store, the world is full of opportunities for anyone ready to step into the realm of income-generating ventures.

The tricky part is figuring out where to start. Many young people aren't sure how to write a good resume or even where to find job openings. It can feel overwhelming when it seems like everyone else has more experience or better connections. And on top of that, balancing school with a job can feel impossible.

But here's the thing: the skills you already possess from school projects, sports teams, and volunteering are more valuable than you think. It's all about showcasing them effectively and managing your time wisely.

In this chapter, we'll guide you through the process of exploring part-time jobs and diving into entrepreneurship. You'll learn how to build a standout resume that highlights your unique experiences, navigate the digital landscape of job searching, and make a lasting impression during interviews. We'll also delve into smart time management strategies to help you balance school and work without burning out. Whether you're aiming to secure that first part-time gig or launch your own small business, we've got practical tips and inspiring stories to set you on the path to success. So, buckle up and get ready to unlock a world of possibilities!

Finding and Securing that First Job

A well-rounded resume can be your golden ticket to landing that first job. It's not just a piece of paper—it's a snapshot of who you are and what you can bring to the table. Even if you've never had an actual job that has paid you money, you've got more relevant skills and experiences than you think. Think about school projects, volunteer work, and any extracurricular activities. Were you the team captain? Did you organize a fundraiser? Have you ever had to babysit your little brother or sister? Those experiences show leadership, initiative, and responsibility.

Here's what you can do to craft an impressive resume:

- Start with a clean, simple layout. Your name and contact information should be at the top.

- Create sections for education, experience, and skills. If you have no work experience, mention relevant classes, school teams or clubs you've been involved in, or summer internships.

- Don't forget your "soft" skills. Communication, teamwork, common sense, and problem-solving abilities are highly valued by employers.

- Use bullet points to list key responsibilities and achievements under each role. Make it easy for someone to quickly scan and see your strengths.

- List your references right on the resume. Your neighbor who's known you for most of your life, your favorite teacher or coach—these references can vouch for your character, work ethic, and skills.

- Check it not once, not twice, but at least THREE times for typos. Show it to someone and get their fresh eyes to look it over. A typo on a resume is a killer. It makes employers doubt your responsibility and seriousness.

When it comes to searching for job opportunities, today's digital landscape offers several platforms designed specifically for young job seekers. Websites like Craigslist, Indeed or Glassdoor can be good starting points, but your school's career center or guidance counselor may have listings or connections with local businesses looking for young talent.

And while those are all great resources, don't underestimate the value of pounding the pavement and going door-to-door to local businesses. It allows you to make a personal connection and leave a strong impression. It shows initiative and determination, and you can directly inquire about job openings, often before they're publicly advertised.

Networking can be a game changer too. You might think networking is something only adults with fancy suits do, but that's not true. It can be very effective for everyone. If you tell your neighbor you're looking for work, they might know someone who's hiring. Talk to teachers, coaches, or even friends' parents—they're often happy to help if they can. And a recommendation from them to a potential employer will go a long way.

To effectively use job search platforms and networking:

- Regularly check job listing websites and set up email alerts for new postings.
- Join local community pages on social media where local job openings are posted.
- Practice your "elevator pitch" so you're prepared to talk about your skills and interests when you meet new people. An elevator pitch is a quick and catchy intro about yourself and your skills. It's called an elevator pitch because it should be short enough to deliver during an elevator ride.
- Once you secure an interview, preparation is key to making a great impression. Interviews can be nerve-wracking, but remember, it's as much about you evaluating if the job is right for you as it is for them getting to know you.

Guidelines for preparing for job interviews:

- Research the company and the position beforehand. Know what the company does, their values, and be aware of any recent news. Is this a company that you want to work for? Now look at the specific job you're applying for. Is this a job you want to do on a regular basis? If you're a germophobe, working in a doctor's office where you'll be exposed to people with illnesses may not be the best idea. If you're interested in law and the legal system, perhaps a local law firm has an entry level clerical position open. If you enjoy talking to and meeting new people, maybe retail is for you.

- Prepare answers for common questions, like "Tell me about yourself" or "Why do you want this job?" Be honest and more importantly, be yourself. Speak from the heart.

- Dress appropriately. Aim for neat and tidy; you don't necessarily need a suit, but avoid overly casual clothes like ripped jeans or graphic tees.

- Bring a copy of your resume and a list of references if they are not included on your resume. It shows you're organized and prepared.

- Show up by yourself. It demonstrates independence, responsibility, and professionalism.

During the interview, professionalism isn't just about what you say, but how you say it and your body language. Make eye contact, offer a firm handshake, and stay relaxed. Confidence speaks louder than words. Don't forget to ask questions too! You can ask about the company, what a typical day looks like in the role and when they plan to make a hiring decision. Perhaps, if time allows, engage the interviewer in a longer discussion by asking them how long they've been with the company. All of these actions show you're really interested in the job.

The process doesn't end once the interview does. Following up after an application or an interview can significantly boost your chances of standing out. While it may feel awkward, it shows initiative and enthusiasm.

Send a thank you email within 24 hours of your interview. Express gratitude for the opportunity and briefly restate your interest in the position. If you haven't heard back within a week or two, you can even send a polite follow-up email expressing your continued interest. Don't forget to keep track of all your applications and follow-ups. A simple spreadsheet can help you stay organized and avoid sending multiple follow-ups to the same employer, or create a folder in your email account to store sent and received communications.

Securing your first job is a milestone, and developing a strong job search strategy can make the process less daunting and more fruitful. It's about presenting yourself well, utilizing resources, preparing thoroughly, and showing persistence. Each step you take builds your confidence and skills, making you more attractive to future employers.

Remember, everyone starts somewhere, and it's okay if things don't go perfectly the first time around. We could fill another book with interview missteps we've made along the way. Treat each experience as a learning opportunity. The effort you put into crafting your resume, networking, preparing for interviews, and following up will set you apart and increase your chances of landing a rewarding part-time position. And will give you an invaluable skillset as you get older.

Balancing School, Work and Self-Care

Balancing school and work can feel like walking a tightrope, especially when you're just starting. But with the right approach, it's totally doable and can help you build a bright future. One key to success is creating a structured and effective schedule.

Creating a structured schedule is key to keep both your academic responsibilities and work commitments in check. Think of your schedule as a blueprint for success. By laying out your tasks, you can visualize what needs to be done and allocate time appropriately. Start by listing all your school assignments, extracurricular activities, and work shifts. Then, slot them into your weekly planner.

Here's what you can do to create an efficient schedule:

- Identify the non-negotiables—these are your school hours and fixed work shifts.
- Break down your study hours and assign specific time blocks for each subject or project.
- Include some downtime. Overloading yourself is a recipe for burnout.
- Review and adjust your schedule regularly. Life happens, and flexibility will help you manage unexpected changes.

A good schedule isn't just about penciling in obligations; it's also about making sure you have time for everything that matters to you.

Sleep, hobbies, and hanging out with friends should all find their place in your plan. When you see everything laid out, it becomes easier to manage your time and ensure you're meeting both your educational and financial goals without sacrificing your well-being.

Now that you've got your schedule, prioritizing tasks is the next step. Not all tasks are created equal, and this is where setting realistic goals comes into play. It's easy to get overwhelmed if you don't know where to start or if you set expectations too high. To prevent this, focus on what's essential and time-sensitive first.

Here are some tips for prioritizing tasks:

- Break down large projects into smaller, manageable chunks. This makes them less daunting and easier to tackle.
- Use tools like to-do lists, calendars, and apps to keep track of your progress and deadlines.
- Set specific, measurable goals for each day. For example, aim to complete one school assignment before heading to your part-time job.
- Be realistic about what you can achieve. It's better to finish fewer tasks well than to take on too much and end up doing things poorly.

Remember, it's okay to ask for help if you're feeling swamped. Whether it's turning to a teacher for guidance or asking a friend for support, leveraging your network can make a huge difference. The key here is not to stretch yourself too thin but to manage your workload in a way that keeps you productive and healthy.

Effective communication with your supervisors at work is another critical piece of the puzzle. Being upfront about your availability and any potential scheduling conflicts can save you a lot of stress. Employers generally appreciate employees who are transparent and proactive about their schedules.

Approach the conversation professionally and politely. Express your commitment to your job but emphasize the importance of your studies. Be sure to provide your availability in advance, highlighting any periods where your schoolwork might be especially intense, such as exam weeks. And of course, always offer possible solutions for any scheduling conflicts, showing that you're thinking ahead and willing to compromise.

Good communication is key. It builds trust and can lead to more flexible working arrangements. Your employer is more likely to accommodate your needs if they understand you're juggling school and work effectively. This doesn't just benefit you; it benefits them as well — it's a win-win situation.

While balancing school and work, self-care often takes a backseat, but it's a crucial element for maintaining a healthy routine. Managing your time efficiently isn't solely about productivity; it's also about ensuring you're not running yourself ragged. Adequate sleep, proper nutrition, regular exercise, and mental health breaks are non-negotiable aspects of taking care of yourself.

Here are some self-care and time management strategies:

- Make sure you're getting enough rest. Aim for at least 7-8 hours of sleep each night. Lack of sleep can severely impact your focus and performance both at school and work.

- Maintain a balanced diet. Skipping meals to save time can lead to energy crashes and reduced efficiency.

- Incorporate physical activity into your routine. Whether it's a quick walk or a workout session, exercise can boost your mood and energy levels.

- Plan for relaxation. Dedicate time each week to activities that help you unwind, like reading, listening to music, or spending quality time with family and friends.

Practicing self-care ensures that you're not only physically fit but also mentally prepared to handle the demands of your schedule. Time management isn't just about fitting everything in—it's about creating a sustainable lifestyle that keeps you going and thriving.

In summary, managing your time efficiently between school and work commitments is achievable with the right approach. Creating a structured schedule provides a clear roadmap for balancing your responsibilities. Prioritizing tasks and setting realistic goals ensures you stay productive without burning out. Effective communication with your supervisors helps you manage your work commitments smoothly. And, most importantly, incorporating self-care into your routine maintains your overall well-being.

Efficient time management is the cornerstone of balancing academic success with part-time work. It allows you to meet your financial goals while excelling in your studies and enjoying a fulfilling life. With these strategies, you'll be able to master this balancing act.

Be Your Own Boss

Starting your own business can be a cool way to take control of your future and do something you're passionate about. Being your own boss means you get to make the decisions, set your own goals, and create something that's truly yours. Whether it's a small side hustle or a big idea, entrepreneurship gives you the freedom to explore your interests and learn valuable skills along the way. In this section, we'll look at some real stories of young people who turned their ideas into successful businesses, proving that you're never too young to start making things happen.

Let's look at Emmi's story. Emmi, at a young age, discovered her love for baking. She didn't wait to finish school to start exploring this passion; instead, at 16 she started baking and selling homemade cookies and cupcakes at local markets, to friends and family and ultimately, online. With nothing more than her mom's kitchen and a Facebook page, Emmi managed to grow her baking business into a buzz-worthy local brand. Her story is not only heartwarming but also incredibly motivating. Here was a teenager, taking an idea and turning it into a real revenue-generating business while still juggling homework and extracurricular activities.

Emmi's journey highlights the significant role that innovation, perseverance, and passion play in entrepreneurial success. She didn't just bake; she created unique flavors and marketed them cleverly on social media. Whenever sales dipped, she came out with a new flavor or tried new marketing strategies. Perseverance meant staying up late to perfect her recipes, even after a long day at school. Emmi's passion for baking kept her going despite challenges—like when she spent six hours straight trying to fix a batch until it turned out right.

Take Christopher, a college student who realized there was a need in his neighborhood for lawn care in the spring, summer and fall and for snow removal in the winter. He took what he normally did at his own house and turned it into a lucrative venture. He noticed that many people were willing to pay good money for snow removal, gutter cleaning and basic lawn care. So, he bought some equipment and decided to go for it – putting up flyers in his neighborhood and posting his services and information online. He constantly improved his skills and customer service. His dedication paid off as he had several happy clients who then went on to refer him to their friends and family and post his phone number on several online neighborhood forums. This, in turn, attracted more business, enabling Christopher to make so much money that he had next semester's tuition saved up in no time!

One of the most significant benefits of being a young entrepreneur in today's market is your familiarity with digital tools and platforms. Many of you are already pros at using social media for personal reasons, but social media can also help you market your products or services. Furthermore, there are countless online resources and communities where you can learn everything from accounting basics to advanced coding skills for your website. But let's not sugarcoat it; challenges will arise. Being a young entrepreneur means balancing school responsibilities with your business. It can be daunting to deal with adult questions about finances or logistics when you're still figuring out algebra. Yet, these experiences offer learning opportunities, turning each challenge into a stepping stone rather than a roadblock.

Innovation in business ideas isn't just limited to profitable projects either. It could be a passion project that will provide you with invaluable lessons for future endeavors, connect you with like-minded individuals and make a good impression on that college application or resume. Katie, a 17-year-old, realized that a lot of teenagers were struggling with mental health issues but found it difficult to seek help. Using her knack for writing and empathy, she created an anonymous online platform where teens could share their stories, connect with one another and even receive advice. The initiative was simple yet powerful and resonated deeply within her peers. Katie's platform grew rapidly, receiving thousands of visitors and even attracting attention from mental health professionals who then began contributing to the space she provided.

Some passion projects can eventually become extremely profitable. In 1995, the very early days of the internet, billionaire Mark Cuban and his friend Todd Wagner took over a streaming company called AudioNet (eventually it became Broadcast.com) simply because they wanted to use the internet to listen to the live radio broadcasts of their alma mater Indiana University's basketball games. Eventually, they developed it so that Broadcast.com offered streaming audio over the internet from other live events too. Streaming was a relatively new concept at the time, and people thought they were crazy. They couldn't understand why this service was needed nor could they see its profitability. But Cuban and Wagner had the last laugh - they sold this passion project just four years later – for 5.7 billion dollars in stock to Yahoo.

These stories highlight essential traits - creativity, resilience, and commitment - that stand behind successful ventures. You don't need a groundbreaking idea to get started. Sometimes, it's about recognizing simple problems around you and crafting a solution or about following a passion. Not every venture will become a million-dollar enterprise. But the skills you gain, the networks you build, and the self-confidence you develop along the way are priceless.

So, what resonates with your interests or needs around you? Perhaps you're an artist, and you could sell custom artwork online or at a local craft fair or marketplace. Do you have a passion for photography? If so, you can take on freelance photography jobs or sell stock photos. If you excel in a particular subject, you can tutor. Love kids? Look into babysitting opportunities in your neighborhood. Are you happiest around your pet? Pet sitting and dog walking can very well be for you! You're on your phone all the time on social media – why not look into managing the social media accounts of small local businesses in your neighborhood, whose owners are clueless about these things. The opportunities are endless if you're willing to explore and innovate. Be creative and find ways to monetize your skills and talents!

The tales of Emmi and Christopher prove that entrepreneurial spirit knows no age limit. It's about seeing opportunities where others see none, learning continuously, and keeping your passion alive even when obstacles arise. Don't let anyone tell you that your youth is a hindrance! It's a unique advantage—you have fresh ideas and a different perspective on the world. If you have a smartphone or a laptop and access to the internet, mix in a little passion, creativity, and hustle – and you have everything you need!

It's easy to feel daunted by the risks and challenges of starting your own venture. Remember that failure is simply another word for "learning experience." Each setback teaches you something valuable, making you wiser and more resilient. Use all resources available to you, from family and friends to mentors and advisors to online courses, Facebook groups and forums. You don't have to do it all alone. Seek guidance and collaborate when necessary.

Pushing yourself towards entrepreneurial endeavors can open doors you never imagined. A mix of passion, innovation, and tenacity can lead to incredible accomplishments—even for those still navigating school corridors. Not only can they become exciting, profitable ventures but they look great on a college application.

When you're diving into the world of making money, whether it's through a part-time job or starting your own small venture, understanding how to manage that money is crucial. So, let's start with the basics we've already discussed: budgeting and saving, and how it applies to a small business venture. Again, we already know that budgeting is about knowing where your money is coming from and deciding where it should go.

First put in place an estimated basic budget - what you think you'll earn and what you think you'll have to spend. In Emmi's case, she can start by estimating how many cookies and/or cupcakes she thinks she can bake and sell in a month and what does it cost her to make and market those sweet treats. Now, it's time to track your actual income and expenses.

Here's a practical approach:

- Use a notebook or a digital app to jot down every penny you earn and spend.
- Review your entries weekly to see if you're coming close to your original estimated budget. This helps you understand your spending patterns and tweak your original budget accordingly.
- Start setting specific financial goals. For instance, you might want to increase sales by $300 each month in your business. Having clear goals gives you something to work towards and can keep you motivated.
- Review and revise: Review your goals. Are they realistic? Are you meeting them? Perhaps setting a smaller goal is more practical and easier to achieve.

Knowing where your money is going and having financial goals can feel incredibly energizing. It builds your confidence and makes you more mindful about your financial decisions.

Risks of Small Business Ventures

We should also discuss the risks as well as the rewards of entrepreneurial ventures. When you're starting out, it's easy to get caught up in the excitement of potentially earning a lot of money, but it's essential to consider both the upsides and downsides.

Any business comes with inherent risks. You might face unexpected costs, market competition, or even failure. However, these risks are often balanced by rewards such as creativity, independence, and the potential for high returns. Understanding this balance helps you make informed decisions and prepares you for potential challenges.

One way to minimize risk is to start small. Test your idea on a smaller scale before investing significant time and money. For example, if you plan to sell handmade crafts, begin by selling to friends or at local markets before expanding. This will help you gauge demand and refine your product without a huge initial investment.

Lastly, never underestimate the value of seeking mentorship or utilizing available resources. Financial mentors can offer insights and guidance that books or online resources simply can't match because they've been there and done that. They provide personalized advice and support, helping you avoid common pitfalls.

Here's how you can connect with mentors:

- Talk to family members or friends who have experience in managing finances or running a business. Tell them your idea and ask for their advice.
- Reach out to teachers, school counselors, or community leaders who might be willing to guide you.
- Join local clubs or online groups focused on entrepreneurship or personal finance or the industry you're looking to enter. Engaging in these communities can provide valuable networking opportunities and resources.

Mentors are invaluable for providing perspective and helping you navigate complex financial decisions. Additionally, there are numerous online resources, webinars, and workshops that can strengthen your understanding of financial management for your business. Just ensure that the resources you use are credible and evidence-based.

Learning how to manage your finances while exploring part-time jobs or entrepreneurial ventures is a vital skill that can set you up for long-term success. By adopting basic financial principles like budgeting and saving, diligently tracking your income and expenses, understanding the financial risks and rewards of your ventures, and seeking guidance from mentors or reliable resources, you're building a strong financial foundation.

Remember, financial literacy is not just about numbers, it's about making informed money management choices. Embrace the journey with an open mind, stay resilient in the face of challenges, and continue seeking knowledge to empower yourself. Your path to financial freedom and entrepreneurial success can start now.

Summary

Your First Step towards Financial Independence

In this journey of exploring income-generating opportunities and entrepreneurial ventures, we've covered a lot. From crafting that perfect resume to nailing job interviews and even managing time between school and work, you now have the tools to confidently step into the workforce. Remember your unique experiences—like leading a school project or organizing a fundraiser—could become assets on your resume. It's all about leveraging what you already know and skills you already have.

Starting early not only builds financial independence but also cultivates essential life skills like responsibility, communication, and problem-solving. You might fumble along the way; maybe your first pitch won't go as planned, or perhaps you'll find balancing tasks a bit overwhelming. And that's okay. Every misstep is just another chance to learn.

The ripple effect of these endeavors can be significant. As more young people embrace part-time jobs or entrepreneurial projects, they collectively contribute to a culture of youth empowerment and innovation. A community filled with young minds eager to solve problems, start businesses, and improve local life is inspiring to think about the potential impact—not just on individual lives but on society as a whole.

So, what's next for you? Will you turn your passion into a side hustle like Emmi's baking business? Take your skills and monetize them like Christopher's lawncare business? Maybe you'll find a different path that excites you just as much. The possibilities are endless, as long as you have the creativity and drive to explore them.

As you venture out, keep in mind that every experience—whether it feels like a win or a setback—is a valuable part of your growth. Take what you've learned, stay curious, and always be open to new opportunities.

CHAPTER 3

MASTERING BUDGETING AND SAVING STRATEGIES

Ever wondered why some people seem to have their financial lives in order while others are constantly scrambling? It might look like some adults have it all figured out and others are always short on cash. But here's the truth: anyone can learn to manage their money wisely. Imagine having enough saved up for that new gadget you want or being able to go on a last minute trip with friends without stressing about how to pay for it. The secret? Mastering budgeting and saving strategies early on.

One of the biggest challenges for many young adults today is figuring out how to handle money effectively. You might get paid from a part-time job or receive some allowance, and before you know it, it's gone on snacks, movies, or a new pair of sneakers. Without a solid plan, it's easy to lose track of where your money goes. Small purchases add up fast, and you might find yourself running short on money at the end of the month if you missed a shift or two at work.

That's why it's crucial to start developing smart habits now, so you can avoid financial stress later in life.

In this chapter, we'll dive into practical tips and strategies for creating personalized budgets and building strong saving habits. You'll learn how to list your income sources, keep tabs on every penny spent, and set realistic spending limits for different categories like food, entertainment, and savings. We'll also explore ways to make budgeting fun and engaging, ensuring it becomes a habit for life rather than a boring chore. By the end, you'll have the tools to take control of your finances and set yourself up for future success.

Mastering the Art of Budgeting

Budgeting may seem like something for adults with mortgages and car payments, but it's a super important skill to master early. It's not just about managing your money today; it's about setting yourself up for financial success in the future. So why not start now? Let's break down budgeting in a way that makes sense and can genuinely make a difference.

First off, let's talk about what budgeting actually is and why it matters. Imagine you're hosting a party and you've got a set amount of snacks. You want to make sure there's enough for everyone throughout the night, so you plan ahead, deciding how much to buy and how to put it out at different times. Budgeting works the same way - it's all about planning where your money goes so you don't run out before you've covered everything important and maybe even saved a little portion for those unexpected emergencies.

Creating a budget might sound complicated, but it doesn't have to be. Here are some steps to get you started:

- List your income: Begin by figuring out where your money comes from. This could be an allowance, a part-time job, or even cash gifts from family members. Write all these down to get a total monthly income.

- Track your expenses: Record every penny you spend. Yes, every single cent. Whether you're buying snacks, paying for a streaming service, or chipping in for gas, jot it all down. This step is crucial because it helps you see where your money goes.

- Set spending limits: Divide your expenses into categories like food, entertainment, savings, and perhaps charity. Set limits for each category based on your income and stick to them. If you realize you're spending too much in one area, it gives you the chance to adjust before you run out of money.

Tracking your expenses might reveal patterns that surprise you. You might find out you're spending half your income on fast food without even realizing it. Or you're spending money on a streaming service that you haven't watched for months. Identifying these patterns is important because it allows you to see where you can cut back.

Once you've set up your budget, don't let it gather dust. A budget isn't a "set it and forget it" thing. Regularly reviewing and adjusting your budget ensures it stays relevant to your life and goals. Just like how you wouldn't keep wearing the same pair of jeans if they no longer fit, don't stick to a budget that doesn't reflect your current situation. Maybe you've started a new job or picked up a new hobby—your budget should change accordingly.

What we've outlined here might seem pretty straightforward, but let's highlight a few key takeaways. First, budgeting is a fundamental skill for financial success. Second, tracking your income and expenses can help you identify those sneaky spending habits. And lastly, regularly reviewing and adjusting your budget is crucial to staying financially stable and achieving your goals.

Learning to budget isn't just about managing the money you have now. It's about building solid habits that will benefit you throughout your life. Knowing how to budget effectively can prevent you from running into debt when you head off to college or start your first full-time job. It's also empowering to know you can save up for big goals like buying a car or going on a trip with friends without having to rely on your parents.

Another tip is to use tools that resonate with your lifestyle. Since most of us are glued to our smartphones, why not use a budgeting app? These apps can help you track your spending in real-time, making it easier to stay within your limits. Plus, seeing your progress can be really motivating. No matter which budgeting tool or app you choose, it's important to find one that works for you.

There are many excellent budgeting apps available such as:

- Mint: You can even connect your bank and credit card accounts and track your spending in real time
- YNAB (You Need a Budget): This app helps you track a progress towards a financial goal

- Personal Capital: This app can also provide you with personalized financial advice based on your individual situation
- EveryDollar: This app helps you allocate each dollar of your income before you spend it.
- PocketGuard: This app has a very simple interface and also can alert you to potential overspending

And remember, your budget isn't set in stone. Life happens. Maybe you need to spend more one month on school supplies or gifts for family and friends. That's okay. The important part is to adjust your budget accordingly and make sure you get back on track afterward.

Savings goals are another aspect of budgeting that's often overlooked. Sure, it's fun to spend money, but saving can be satisfying too, especially when you know it's for something special. Set specific goals, like saving for a new bike, a new car, a summer trip, or even just a rainy day fund. Having a clear goal can make it easier to say no to unnecessary purchases because you know you're working towards something bigger.

Remember that balancing personal responsibility with the need for a safety net is key. It's great to be responsible and mindful of your spending, but don't be too hard on yourself if you make mistakes. Everyone does. What's important is learning from those mistakes and continuing to improve your budgeting skills. There's a reason why budgeting is considered a lifelong skill—it takes time and practice to get it right.

Lastly, talk to someone experienced about your budget. This could be a parent, older sibling, or even a teacher. They can offer valuable insights and possibly share some of their own experiences. Sometimes an outside perspective can provide clarity on areas you might miss.

Mastering the art of budgeting sets the stage for a lifetime of financial health and freedom. It's a blend of understanding your income, tracking your expenses, setting realistic goals, and regularly tweaking your plan to fit your evolving needs. Embrace it early on, and you'll find yourself better prepared for whatever financial challenges come your way. Plus, there's a certain confidence that comes with knowing you're in control of your finances.

Effective Savings Strategies

Now, let's dive into how you can set meaningful savings goals and make sure your money works for you.

First off, setting specific saving goals is crucial. Think about what you want to save for—maybe it's a new phone, college, or that epic summer trip. Having clear goals helps you stay motivated and focused. Here is what you can do in order to achieve the goal:

- Start by writing down what you're saving for and how much it will cost.
- Break it down into smaller milestones. If your goal is big, like saving $1,000, divide it into manageable chunks, such as $100 every month.
- Set a deadline for each milestone to keep yourself on track.

- Keep these goals somewhere visible, like your phone calendar or a sticky note on your mirror, to remind yourself daily.

Next, let's talk about strategies. Saving money can be challenging but automating your savings makes it easier. Automatic transfers are a lifesaver. Set up an automatic transfer from your checking to your savings account right after you get paid. This way, you don't even have to think about it; the money is saved before you're tempted to spend it. Maybe even consider setting up a dedicated savings account specifically for your goals; having separate accounts can help you resist the urge to dip into your savings for non-essential items.

Another fun strategy is participating in savings challenges. There are plenty out there, like the 52-week challenge where you increase your savings amount each week. It's surprisingly motivating to see those small amounts add up over time. Alternatively, use savings apps that round up your purchases to the nearest dollar and save the difference. You will be amazed at how quickly spare change accumulates without any extra effort.

Speaking of safety nets, let's highlight the benefits of building an emergency fund. Life is unpredictable. Cars break down, phones get lost, or sudden medical bills appear. An emergency fund acts as your financial buffer, keeping you afloat when these unplanned expenses hit. Aim to have enough to cover three to six months' worth of your expenses. That might sound like a lot, but remember, it doesn't need to happen overnight. Start with small, consistent contributions, no matter how minimal.

Most financial experts suggest starting with a goal of $1,000. It's a tangible target and a great first step towards building a more substantial cushion. Once you hit that initial goal, continue adding to it until you reach that three to six-month benchmark.

Now, imagine the peace of mind you'll have knowing you're financially prepared for unexpected events. A recent NerdWallet survey noted that while a majority of Americans have some form of savings, nearly half can't even cover an unexpected $1,000 expense. Having an emergency fund means you won't be quick to reach for a credit card and fall into debt when life throws you a curveball.

Saving consistently isn't just about emergencies; it's also key to achieving long-term objectives. Let's say you start putting aside just $50 a month. By the end of the year, that's $600! Compound that over a few years, and you've not only got a solid emergency fund but also funds for future projects and dreams. Consistent saving habits build financial security, giving you freedom and control over your life choices.

And speaking of choice, let's not forget the sense of accomplishment that comes with meeting your financial goals. It's empowering to see your savings grow and to know you've built that with your own efforts. Plus, this sets you up with valuable habits that will benefit you throughout your life.

Here are a few additional tips to keep your savings journey smooth:

- Avoid lifestyle inflation. Just because you get a raise or windfall, like birthday cash, doesn't mean you need to spend more. Stick to your budget and increase your savings instead.

- Periodically review your savings goals and adjust them as needed. Life changes, and so do your aspirations. Stay flexible.

- Celebrate progress. When you hit a milestone, give yourself a little reward. It's important to acknowledge your hard work and stay motivated.

Setting clear savings goals helps you prioritize your financial objectives and makes it easier to achieve them. Consistent saving habits also build financial stability, giving you both peace of mind and long-term security. And having an emergency fund? That's your lifeline when things go wrong. It ensures you can handle unexpected expenses without throwing your finances off track. Be empowered, be informed, and be resilient. Start budgeting and building those saving habits today, and you'll see how it changes your tomorrow.

When it comes to creating effective budgets and cultivating saving habits, there are ways to make the process fun and rewarding. There are several creative techniques that can help make saving money an enjoyable experience.

First up, introducing a game element can significantly incentivize saving behaviors. Incorporate elements of games—like point systems, quests, and leaderboards—into non-game activities. It's like turning saving money into a game where you earn points or levels. To get started:

- Create a savings game: Set up a system where you can put up a chart on your wall, tracking your progress. Seeing how close you are getting to your goal can boost motivation.

- Develop quests: These quests could be mini-challenges related to saving, such as finding deals when shopping or setting aside a certain amount each week. Completing these quests could unlock rewards like extra pocket money or a special treat.

- Introduce leaderboards: If you have siblings or friends, create a friendly competition by putting up a leaderboard to see who can save the most in a month. A little competition can make the process more exciting and engaging.

Studies show that gamification engages both intrinsic and extrinsic motivation, providing pleasure in the activity itself and external rewards.

Another fun idea is to set up saving challenges or competitions with friends or family members. Challenges can keep the momentum going and make saving a social activity rather than a solitary one.

Here's how you can do this:

- Saving races: Set a goal, like saving $50 by the end of the month, and see who gets there first. The winner gets bragging rights, but everyone wins by saving money.

- Themed challenges: Try thematic savings challenges, such as a "no-spend weekend" where participants refrain from spending any money over the weekend.

- Family savings projects: Families can work together to save money for a common goal, such as a vacation or a new gadget. Each family member contributes what they can, turning it into a collective effort and a bonding experience.

Lastly, discussing the psychological benefits of associating positive emotions with saving money is essential. When one feels good about their saving efforts, it fosters a healthy financial mindset. We'll discuss the importance of mindset later on in the book but simply put, our emotions drive a lot of our decisions, including those related to money.

By celebrating each success, no matter how small, you can start to connect saving money with positive feelings. This positive reinforcement can lead to consistent saving habits because the act of saving feels rewarding in itself.

In essence, making saving fun can give you the boost you need to stay motivated and consistent. By integrating gamification, setting up challenges, rewarding progress, and fostering positive associations, you can transform the difficult task of saving money into an engaging and fulfilling task.

Turn saving into an adventure - one where every dollar saved is a step towards victory. Whether it's through leveling up in a personalized savings game or celebrating milestones with rewards, the journey is just as important as the destination. And remember, it's okay to make mistakes along the way; each error is just a learning opportunity in disguise.

Distinguishing Between Needs and Wants

Distinguishing between needs and wants isn't just some grown-up jargon - it's a skill that can shape your entire financial future.

Going through the maze of what you absolutely must have versus what would be nice to have is foundational in creating an effective budget.

First, let's talk about essential expenses. Simply put, these are the non-negotiables - you can't live without them. These are your needs. We're talking food, rent or mortgage, utilities, and transportation whether it's a car payment and insurance or fares for public transportation. Of course, it can also include things like health insurance and season-appropriate clothing.

Discretionary spending covers everything else that adds comfort or enjoyment but isn't crucial for survival. These are wants. Some examples of wants are going to the movies, eating out, or buying the latest new phone even though your old one is working just fine.

Sometimes, what's considered a need for one person might be a want for another. Take, for example, a car. If you live in an area with frequent and reliable public transportation, owning a car might not be a necessity. On the other hand, if you're in a rural area where there is no local bus or train, a vehicle becomes essential. It's also fluid - what you need today might become a want tomorrow and vice versa as your circumstances change.

So, how do you evaluate which is which? Here's where we dive into some practical tips:

- Question its necessity: Ask yourself, "Do I really need this to live and function?" If the answer is no, it's most likely a want.

- Pause before purchase: Hold off on buying items immediately. The pull for a genuine need will grow stronger over time, while a want may lose its luster.
- Explore cheaper alternatives: Sometimes a need can be fulfilled in a less expensive way. Always shop around, and look for sales or coupons.
- Reflect on its impact: Think about how different your life would be without that item. If it won't make a significant impact, it's probably a want.

Once you've categorized your expenses, you can move on to creating a practical budget plan.

Making informed spending decisions is not just about categorizing needs and wants—it's about prioritizing your spending based on individual values and goals. Here's how you can go about doing that:

- Identify your values: Know what's important to you. Maybe it's education, health, or even saving for a car or future travel.
- Align your spending: Prioritize spending on things that align closely with your values.
- Set clear goals: Whether it's saving for college, a car, or even a big trip, having clear financial goals helps filter out unnecessary expenditures.
- Track and review: Regularly monitor your spending to ensure you're still aligned with your values and goals.

Delayed gratification is a concept that's worth understanding. It's all about waiting for better rewards rather than going for instant pleasure. When you delay gratification, you're making a conscious choice to hold off on smaller, immediate rewards in favor of larger, long-term benefits. This might mean saving up for six months to buy a high-quality laptop rather than splurging on a less efficient one right away. Studies show that individuals who practice delayed gratification often experience better financial stability later in life. So how can you incorporate it into your budgeting habits?

- Create a wish list: Instead of impulsively buying something, add it to a wish list and revisit it after a month. Often, you'll find that many items don't seem as appealing even just a month later.
- Visualize long-term goals: Keep a visual representation of your bigger financial goals—like a photo of that dream car, university or destination. Every time you're tempted to spend on a whim, look at it.
- Reward yourself wisely: It's okay to indulge occasionally but make sure it's balanced. Small rewards here and there can keep you motivated without derailing your bigger plans.

Let's take a look at some scenarios where distinguishing between needs and wants can lead to smarter budget allocation and increased savings. Let's say you're planning to hang out with friends, and you're torn between going out to see a movie or watching one at home with everyone bringing snacks. Watching a movie at home significantly reduces costs and lets you save more money for a bigger goal, like buying a car or traveling.

Another scenario is choosing between buying lunch every day or meal-prepping at home. While the convenience of grabbing a quick bite might seem attractive, prepping meals can save you a considerable sum over time.

Ultimately, breaking down your needs and wants isn't just about cutting back on expenses; it's about making conscious choices that are in line with your long-term objectives. Understanding the difference between needs and wants lays the foundation for achieving your financial goals. Practicing delayed gratification encourages better decision-making, and smart budget allocation allows you to streamline your resources efficiently.

It's all about making those conscious choices, learning to pause and reflect, then acting according to your goals. Once you master this, you'll find that your financial habits become healthier, setting you up for greater financial security and freedom in the future. Remember, making conscious spending decisions doesn't mean you completely deprive yourself of life's pleasures. It means you control your finances in a way that aligns with your long-term goals. Practicing these habits now will set you up for success, giving you the power to navigate your financial future with confidence.

One practical method to keep your budget on track is using the 50/30/20 rule. This guideline suggests dividing your income as follows:

- 50% for needs (like gas or your phone bill)
- 30% for wants (like going to a concert or eating out)
- 20% for savings and debt repayment

If you follow this rule, you ensure that you're covering your essentials, enjoying your money, and saving for the future all at the same time.

Summary

Achieving Financial Empowerment through Smart Budgeting and Saving

We've gone through why budgeting matters, explained how to track income and expenses, and discussed the importance of reviewing and adapting your budget over time. We've also explored strategies like the 50/30/20 rule, using budgeting apps, and understanding the difference between needs and wants.

Budgeting isn't just important for today but sets you up for lifelong financial success. Mastering these skills early on has tremendous benefits. It helps prevent debt when you move on to bigger responsibilities, like college or your first apartment, and gives you the confidence to make informed financial decisions.

Some readers might feel overwhelmed by all these steps and strategies. It's perfectly normal to feel this way—starting something new often feels challenging. But remember, every expert was once a beginner. The key is to start small and build from there. Even if you only begin by tracking your expenses or setting aside a tiny amount each month, you're already making progress.

So, what's the takeaway here? Budgeting isn't just about dollars and cents; it's about dollars and sense! It's about planning for your life. As you continue your financial journey, think of your budget as a map guiding you toward your goals. Revisit and revise it as needed, always keeping your bigger picture in sight.

In the end, it's not just about the numbers. It's about the sense of control and empowerment that comes from knowing you're prepared for whatever comes your way. So take that first step, however small it might be, and watch how your financial confidence grows. Remember, your future self will thank you.

Chapter 4

Smart Credit Management

U nderstanding how credit works early on will set the foundation for a strong financial future and help you avoid drowning in debt. In this chapter, we'll break down everything you need to know about using credit cards wisely and the importance of establishing a solid credit history. We'll cover the basics: what a credit limit is, why it's crucial to track your credit utilization and credit reports, and practical tips like making on-time payments and understanding the impact of interest rates. You'll learn how to avoid the biggest common pitfall – overspending!

Let's talk about a common problem that happens when people don't understand credit: debt. For example, you get a shiny new credit card with a $1,000 limit. It's exciting, and at first, it feels like free money. So, you start buying things—some cool sneakers, a ticket to a concert, the latest video game — and before you know it, your card is maxed out. Not only do you owe the bank $1,000, but they're also charging you interest every month on what you owe. If you only make the minimum payment, it'll take ages to pay off, and you'll end up paying much more than you borrowed. And if you miss any minimum payments? Well, that's like hitting a giant pothole on the road to good credit; it damages your credit score and makes future borrowing more difficult and expensive.

Understanding How Credit Cards Work and Building a Positive Credit History

Knowing how credit cards work and building a positive credit history can completely change your financial future for the better. Credit cards are super convenient, and if you use them responsibly, they'll help you build a strong credit score. But without the right understanding, they can also lead you straight into uncontrollable and suffocating debt.

They can be a double-edged sword for young adults if not managed properly. While they offer opportunities to build a positive credit history, misuse can lead to significant financial challenges. It's important to understand how credit cards work and how you can leverage them responsibly to set yourself up for future success.

First, it's crucial to understand the concept of credit limits and utilization. Your credit limit is the maximum amount of "trust" a bank has in you. It's the maximum amount of money the bank is willing to lend you. Credit utilization ratio is simply how much you've used versus your total credit limit. For example, if your credit card has a $1,000 limit and you have charged $300 on it, you've used 30% of your credit. Keeping this ratio low is important because higher utilization ratios can signal to lenders that you might be overextending yourself – basically taking on too much debt than you can handle. By understanding this concept, you can manage your balances more responsibly and build a stronger financial foundation.

Once you have a credit card, you'll start building a credit report and a credit score. A credit report is exactly what it sounds like - it's a record of your credit history. It includes what credit cards and loans you have, how much you owe and whether you pay the bills on time. A credit score is a numerical representation of your creditworthiness, showing how likely you are to repay borrowed money. It's derived from the information on your credit report. Your credit score is based on factors like payment history, amounts owed, length of credit history, types of credit, and new accounts. Overall, your credit score is a combination of these factors and typically ranges from 300 to 850. Most consumers have credit scores that fall between 600 and 750. 700 or above is generally considered good. 800 or above is considered to be excellent. A higher credit score indicates responsible financial behavior and can lead to better loan terms, lower interest rates, and easier access to credit.

Credit scores are calculated by credit bureaus or credit reporting agencies. The three main ones are Equifax, Experian, and TransUnion. These agencies collect information from lenders, credit card companies, and other financial institutions about your balances, borrowing and repayment habits. Using sophisticated algorithms - complex mathematical formulas or sets of rules that are designed to process large amounts of data and make calculations or decisions based on that data - each bureau generates a credit score based on the data in your credit report. While the basic principles of credit scoring are similar across agencies, slight variations in scoring models and the data used can result in slightly different scores from each bureau.

Credit card companies and other lenders then view your credit report and credit score to make a determination about you. Will they give you more credit? How much more? And of course, what will be your Annual Percentage Rate (APR)? The more positive information that is in your credit report, the better the result will be for you. Those who have better credit histories will get more favorable terms.

Now, let's talk about timely payments. One of the most impactful actions you can take to maintain and build your credit score is making payments on time. Think about your payment history like your academic report card—it showcases whether you've been reliable or not. Even if you miss just one payment, it can have negative consequences on your credit report for years. This simple action of paying on time every month demonstrates responsibility and reliability, which are key traits lenders look for. You should always set up automatic payments from your bank account, or at the very least, use electronic reminders to ensure you never miss a due date. These small steps can make a world of difference and help you maintain a high credit score.

Missing payments or carrying a high balance can seriously hurt your credit score. When you miss a payment, not only do you incur late fees, but your credit score takes a hit as well. High balances relative to your credit limit can also hurt your credit utilization ratio. Imagine you're at the end of a school term and your report card shows a significant drop in grades because of one bad test score—that's similar to what happens to your credit score when you miss payments or carry high balances. To avoid these pitfalls, it's essential to manage your credit card wisely:

- Set reminders for due dates. Better yet, set up automatic payments for at least the minimum on the due date in case you miss it.
- Pay more than the minimum payment if possible.
- If you find it hard to keep track, consolidate your balance to fewer cards.

By doing so, you demonstrate responsible usage and help elevate your credit standing.

Understanding the credit utilization ratio and keeping it low is another critical aspect. As mentioned earlier, the ratio reflects how much of your available credit you're using. Lenders generally prefer to see this number below 30%. Lower ratios indicate lower risk. For example, if your total available credit across all your cards is $5,000 and you owe $1,000, your utilization ratio is 20%, which is excellent. Here are some practical tips to manage this effectively:

- Aim to use your credit card for essential purchases only.
- Pay off your balance periodically rather than waiting until the end of the billing cycle.
- Keep your old accounts open even if you don't use them often, as they contribute to your total available credit and look better as they establish longer credit history.

By following these guidelines, you'll show lenders that you're using your credit responsibly, building a stronger credit profile over time.

One last tip - always review your credit report. Just like reviewing feedback on homework or tests helps you improve, checking your credit report lets you catch errors or unauthorized transactions. In the United States, you are entitled to one free credit report annually from each of the three major credit bureaus: Equifax, Experian, and TransUnion. You can easily access these reports through AnnualCreditReport.com, the only authorized source for free credit reports, and more and more banks and credit card companies offer free reporting in their app or on their website. By reviewing your credit report regularly, you can spot any errors or signs of identity theft early on, ensuring that your credit history remains accurate and your credit score stays strong.

Understanding how credit cards work and utilizing them responsibly is pivotal in building a solid credit history. Making timely payments, managing your credit utilization ratio, and regularly reviewing your credit report will set you on the right path. Remember, your goal should always be to demonstrate responsibility and reliability, both of which will pay off immensely in the long run when you try to buy a car, rent an apartment or even when you get auto insurance.

Identifying Warning Signs of Credit Card Debt and Strategies for Prevention

Let's talk about something critical for your financial future: responsible credit card usage and debt avoidance. Picture this: you're shopping online, and that cool gadget you've been eyeing is just one click away. Using a credit card makes it so easy but with that comes a responsibility to keep your spending in check.

First up, it's essential to recognize the signs of overspending and accumulating credit card debt. We all know how tempting it can be to splurge on things we love, but consistently spending beyond your means can quickly spiral into debt. A handy strategy to avoid this is tracking your spending habits. Think about setting up a simple budget tracker on your phone or jotting down each purchase in a notebook. Another effective method is to save up for purchases instead of swiping your card impulsively.

Here are some tactics you might find helpful:

- Track every expenditure: Whether it's a fancy cup of coffee or a new pair of sneakers, write it down or input it into an app. This helps visualize where your money goes.
- Set spending limits: Decide on a monthly limit for non-essential spends, like entertainment or dining out, and stick to it.
- Prepay your card: Consider making payments to your credit card whenever you get paid, based on anticipated monthly expenses. This way, you won't be caught off guard by end-of-month bills.

Now, let's move on to understanding the impact of minimum payments and high-interest rates. When you see the bill come through, the minimum payment might seem like a nice lifeline - just pay a small amount, and you're good, right? Not really. Paying only the minimum can lead to long-term debt due to insanely high interest rates. Instead, aim to pay more than the minimum amount due each month, which significantly reduces the interest you'll accrue and helps clear your debt faster.

Here's what you can do:

- Pay more than the minimum: Even if it's just a little extra, paying above the minimum can drastically reduce your debt over time.

- Target high-interest cards first: If you have multiple cards, focus on paying off those with the highest interest rate first. This approach minimizes the total interest you pay.

- Avoid new charges: Until you've managed to pay off your balance, put a temporary halt on using the card except for emergencies.

Next, it's vital to discuss the consequences of maxing out your credit cards. Using up all of your available credit can lead to a vicious cycle of debt that's tough to escape. Maxing out increases your credit utilization ratio. It can damage your credit score but also leaves little room for unexpected expenses. Sometimes, it can even increase your interest rate. Use your credit responsibly to avoid such financial burdens.

Think of these tips:

- Keep utilization low: Again, aim to use only 30% of your available credit limit. For example, if your limit is $1,000, try to keep your balance below $300.

- Emergency buffer: Always keep some credit available for unforeseen circumstances.

- Stay accountable: Share your financial goals with someone you trust who can help keep you on track.

Finally, knowing where to turn for help is empowering. Many young people are unaware of the resources available for debt management and financial counseling. Seeking advice is a proactive step towards addressing credit card debt issues before they get out of hand.

Resources you could explore include:

- Credit counseling services: Nonprofit organizations offer free sessions to help you develop a debt management plan tailored to your needs.
- Financial workshops: Look for local and online workshops specifically designed for teens and young adults.
- Peer support: Sometimes discussing your challenges with friends or family members who understand can provide valuable insights and encouragement.

Being aware of warning signs and taking preventive measures are pivotal to your financial health. Imagine getting through college, starting your first job, and already having a firm grip on managing your finances; it sets you up for a stress-free and promising future.

To sum up, here are the key takeaways: track your spending diligently, always aim to pay more than the minimum on your credit card bills, avoid maxing out your credit cards, and don't hesitate to seek professional financial counsel when needed. By following these guidelines, you'll build a strong foundation for financial well-being, allowing you to enjoy the benefits of a credit card without falling into the trap of endless debt.

Remember, being smart and disciplined with your credit today ensures a brighter and financially secure tomorrow.

Exploring the Costs and Benefits of Using Credit Cards Wisely

Navigating the world of credit cards can seem complex, but understanding both their benefits and risks is crucial for making smart financial choices. Let's explore the different facets of using credit cards wisely and how you can avoid falling into debt traps.

First, let's talk about the advantages of using credit cards. Sure, they offer unparalleled convenience - you don't need to carry around wads of cash, and they are widely accepted. Moreover, responsibly using a credit card helps build your credit history, which is invaluable when it's time for student loans, car loans, or even mortgages in the future. But there's a flip side. Credit cards can also be risky if not managed carefully. Overspending is a common problem. It's easy to swipe now and think about the cost later, but those purchases add up quickly. Add interest charges to the mix, and you could find yourself in a cycle of debt that's hard to escape.

We would be remiss if we didn't mention rewards programs and cashback offers. These features can be enticing. Who wouldn't want to earn points or get some money back on purchases they were going to make anyway? However, it's key to remember that these perks should enhance your financial well-being, not detract from it. Here's what you can do to maximize these benefits responsibly:

- Opt for cards with no or low annual membership fees that offer rewards relevant to your spending habits.

- Pay off your credit card balance in full each month to avoid interest charges that could nullify any cashback or rewards earned.
- Keep an eye on your spending to ensure you're not overspending just to earn rewards.

Next, let's discuss annual membership fees, interest rates, and penalties associated with credit cards. Understanding these costs is vital for selecting the right card. High-interest rates can significantly increase the amount you owe if you carry a balance month-to-month, turning a small purchase into a much larger expense over time. Penalties for late payments or exceeding your credit limit can also add up swiftly.

To choose a card with favorable terms:

- Compare different cards by looking at the Annual Percentage Rate (APR) and any associated fees. There are plenty of credit card options out there for no or low membership fees.
- Read reviews and research whether the card fits your lifestyle and financial goals. For example, cards that offer cash back may be a better option for you than ones that offer miles.
- Use online comparison tools to see side-by-side evaluations of various credit cards.

Lastly, one often overlooked aspect is thoroughly reading and understanding credit card agreements and statements. These documents can be dense and filled with jargon, but they contain crucial information about your responsibilities and potential costs.

Empowering yourself with this knowledge ensures you won't be blindsided by unexpected fees.

Here's how to tackle it:

- Take your time to read through the terms and conditions before signing up for a card.
- Regularly check your statements to track your spending and spot any unauthorized transactions or mistakes.
- If you're ever confused about specific terms or details, don't hesitate to ask for clarification from your card issuer, a trusted adult, or do some research online.

Understanding the costs and benefits of using credit cards effectively prepares you to leverage these financial tools wisely. By maximizing rewards, choosing the right cards, staying informed about terms, and keeping spending in check, you can build a solid credit history without falling into debt traps.

Strategies to Maintain a Healthy Credit Score for Future Financial Endeavors

Now, on to the fascinating world of credit scores! It might not sound thrilling at first, but this stuff is super important and can make a big difference in your future.

First up, let's talk about what actually makes up your credit score. Think of your credit score like your GPA—it's a way for lenders to see how good you are at managing money. The big factors that play into your credit score are payment history, credit utilization, and credit mix.

Payment history is all about whether you pay your bills on time. This is the most important part. Lenders want to see that you're reliable. Credit utilization is basically how much of your available credit you're using. Again, aim to keep it below 30%, so if your credit limit is $1,000, try not to go over $300. Lastly, credit mix looks at the different types of credit you have—credit cards, car loans, student loans, etc. A nice variety shows that you can handle different financial responsibilities.

Monitoring these aspects can improve your credit score and thereby, your creditworthiness. It's like keeping an eye on your grades throughout the semester so there are no surprises at the end. Regularly check your credit report to make sure everything looks right. Again, you can get one free report per year from each of the three major bureaus (Equifax, Experian, and TransUnion) at AnnualCreditReport.com. If something doesn't look right, take action immediately to fix it.

If you find errors, here's what you can do to dispute them and set things straight:

- First, identify the error. Make sure it really is a mistake and not a forgotten bill or an unpaid fine.
- Gather any relevant documents that support your claim. This could be bank statements, receipts, or emails.
- Contact the credit bureau where the error appears. Write a letter explaining the mistake clearly and attach copies of your supporting documents.
- Follow up. Keep track of your claim and ensure that the bureau is taking the necessary steps to correct the error.

Advocating for your credit reputation is crucial. Don't just let mistakes slide, but rather stand up for your financial credibility. If you spot inaccuracies and think "oh well," it could cost you heavily in the long run. You have a right to insist that your credit report contains accurate information. You can get more information about your rights regarding your credit on the Consumer Financial Protection Bureau's website at: www.consumerfinance.gov/learnmore.

Now, why should you even bother with all this? What's the big deal about having a good credit score? Well, maintaining a solid credit score has many long-term benefits. A good credit score can get you loans with low interest rates – you get better deals because you've shown you're responsible. You'll also have an easier time getting approved for mortgages or car loans, which means more freedom and options when you're ready to make those big purchases. It's about setting yourself up for success down the road.

So, to stay on top of this, let's introduce some tools and resources that can help you monitor your credit. Credit monitoring tools are like having a personal finance coach who keeps tabs on your progress. These tools alert you to changes in your credit report, help you understand your credit score better, and can even provide tips on how to improve it.

Here's how you can start:

- Sign up for a credit monitoring service. Some banks and credit card companies offer this for free, or you can choose a paid service for more features.

- Set alerts for suspicious activity. This helps you catch any potential fraud early.
- Regularly review your credit reports. Make it a habit to check your credit report every six months to ensure everything is accurate.
- Use financial management apps that link to your accounts to give you a comprehensive view of your finances.

Staying vigilant and proactive in managing your credit profiles will ensure that you're always one step ahead. It's a bit like doing regular maintenance on your car - ignoring small issues could lead to bigger problems down the line.

Always remember that maintaining a healthy credit score is essential for accessing future financial opportunities. Starting now with good habits helps secure your financial stability later. By managing your credit wisely, you're not only safeguarding your present but also investing in your future.

So, next time you swipe that card or consider applying for a new one, think about how it affects your credit score. Just like working hard to keep your GPA up, taking care of your credit score pays off in the long run.

Most Common Credit Score Myths

There are also many misconceptions about credit scores. For example, many people believe that checking their credit score will hurt their credit score, but this is simply not true. Checking your credit score is known as a "soft inquiry," and it has no impact on your credit score. Soft inquiries are different from "hard inquiries" which occur when you apply for credit. And while hard inquiries can temporarily lower your credit score, soft inquiries have no effect. In fact, it's smart to check it regularly to make sure there are no mistakes or signs of fraud.

Another common myth is that only those with long credit histories can have a good credit score. Now, while it's true that a longer credit history can help your credit score, it's not a requirement. It's possible to have a good credit score with a shorter credit history if you use credit responsibly and pay your bills on time.

The one we hear most often is that people think they must have a perfect credit score. First, there's no such thing as a perfect credit score, and you can still be approved for credit or get good interest rates with a good score. While a high credit score is great, it's more important to focus on using credit responsibly and paying your bills on time. As long as you're doing those things, you don't need to worry about having a perfect credit score.

Summary

Implementing Your Credit Card Strategy

We've covered a lot about responsible credit card use and how to avoid the pitfalls of debt. We started with understanding how credit cards work—credit limits, utilization ratios, and the importance of timely payments. Think of your credit limit as the trust a bank places in you. Keeping your spending within that limit shows reliability.

Next, we identified the warning signs of overspending and accumulating debt. Just like how unchecked snacking can lead to a sugar rush and a subsequent crash, uncontrolled spending can spiral into debt. Tracking expenses, setting spending limits, and paying more than the minimum balance are useful strategies to avoid those financial headaches.

We also looked at the pros and cons of credit cards—from the convenience and rewards to the looming danger of high-interest rates and penalties. Remember that cool gadget or new shoes? Sure, they're tempting, but the interest on impulsive buys can quickly turn them into regrettable expenses. Choosing cards wisely by comparing terms and thoroughly understanding agreements helps in avoiding these traps.

Finally, we delved into maintaining a healthy credit score. Your credit score is essentially your financial GPA. Aiming to keep a low credit utilization ratio and monitoring your credit report regularly ensures that you keep this score in good standing. Regular checks help flag errors or fraud before they become bigger problems.

So, here's the thing: using credit cards isn't inherently bad; it's how you use them that counts. Mismanagement can lead to long-term financial stress, just like cramming for exams last minute isn't a great idea for your grades. By staying vigilant, being smart about how you use your credit and making informed decisions, you're setting yourself up for a brighter financial future.

Building credit takes time and consistency. Pay your bills on time, use your credit responsibly, and keep your balances low. Before you know it, you will have a solid credit history and a strong score to match.

Stay mindful, stay proactive, and remember, each responsible choice you make now builds a better financial foundation for the future. Take charge of your credit and show the world how capable you are.

CHAPTER 5

INTRODUCTION TO INVESTING AND WEALTH BUILDING

Investing is like planting a seed today that will grow into a massive, fruit-bearing tree in the future. It may feel like a distant concept now, but starting early can reshape your financial future in incredible ways. Whether you've got a part-time job or just some birthday money stashed away, putting even a tiny bit into investments can set you up for huge gains down the road. Think of it as giving yourself a gift that keeps on growing.

Many young people don't start investing early because they either don't understand how it works or think it's only for adults. But investing early has great benefits. Take, for example, the concept of compound interest. If you invest $1,000 at an annual interest rate of 5%, by the end of the first year, you would have $1,050. In the second year, your $1,050 earns another 5%, giving you $1,102.50. As time goes on, your money makes money on itself, growing exponentially rather than linearly. It's like planting a seed and watching it turn into a forest over the years. Yet, without knowing this, many miss out on on these benefits simply because they had not planted their financial "trees" early enough.

In this chapter, we'll cover the basics you need to kickstart your investment journey. We'll explore different types of investments like stocks, bonds, and mutual funds, and how they can help you to grow your wealth. We'll touch on cryptocurrency investing – what is it, and what are its pros and cons. You'll learn about risk and return, diversification, and the magic of long-term strategies like dollar-cost averaging. By the end, you'll have a clear roadmap for making informed decisions that can secure your financial future, setting you on a path toward true financial independence. Ready to get started? Let's plant those seeds of wealth!

Understanding Basic Investment Concepts and Compound Interest

When looking into the world of investments and financial growth, one of the most crucial concepts to get under your belt is compound interest. It's like a growing tree. Over time, that tree doesn't just grow straight up; it branches out, each new branch growing more branches until it becomes a massive oak. Compound interest works similarly but with money.

Compound interest is one of those financial concepts that can genuinely change your life. Here's how it works: when you invest money, you earn interest on your initial investment. Over time, that interest also starts earning interest – so the money you earned makes even more money for you.

Compound interest makes your money grow exponentially over time. For example, if you invest $1,000 at 5% interest, after one year, you would have $1,050. The next year, both your initial $1,000 and the extra $50 will earn interest. By year two, you'll have $1,102.50. This might seem like a small increase initially, but stretched over decades, the difference becomes monumental. Even small contributions can balloon into significant amounts given enough time. The key takeaway here? Start investing as soon as you can. The earlier you start, the more you benefit from the magic of compounding interest.

Now, let's look at some of the ways you can start investing. Stocks, bonds, and mutual funds are some of the most common ways to put your money to work. Stocks represent ownership in a company. When the company does well, so do you. Bonds, on the other hand, are like loans you give to companies or the government; in return, they pay you interest. Mutual funds pool money from many investors to buy a diversified mix of stocks, bonds, or other securities. Each of these comes with its own set of risks and rewards.

Understanding risk and return is another critical factor in making smart investments. High-risk investments (like individual stocks) offer the potential for high returns, but they can also result in significant losses. Lower-risk investments (like government bonds) provide more stability but typically offer lower returns. A balanced portfolio - one that includes different types of investments - can help mitigate risks. This approach is known as diversification. Think of it as not putting all your eggs in one basket. By spreading your money across different types of investments, you reduce the risk of one bad investment dragging down and hurting your entire portfolio.

Time and again, we see that starting early, diversifying your investments, and understanding risk and return are critical steps for financial growth. So, what's the game plan? First, don't delay. The sooner you start, the better off you'll be in the long run. Second, make sure your investments are varied to cushion against market volatility. Third, grasp that higher returns usually come with higher risk, and balance your investment choices accordingly.

Remember, the road to financial growth isn't a sprint; it's a marathon. With patience, consistency, and an informed strategy, anyone can harness the power of compound interest to secure their financial future.

Comparison of Different Beginner Investments

Investment can also be like planting a garden – some plants grow fast and tall, and others take their time but are sturdy. Knowing the risk levels of these plants is just as important as knowing how to water them.

When it comes to investment risks, think of stocks like roses in a garden – they can bloom beautifully or get caught in the thorns. Stocks are shares in a company, meaning you own a tiny piece of that business. They have high potential returns but also come with significant risks. One day your stocks could be enjoying the sunshine, growing strong; the next, they might wilt if the market takes a downturn. For instance, back in 2012, Facebook shares started at $38 but plummeted to $18.05 within three months.

On the other hand, bonds are like dependable sunflowers – they grow slowly and steadily. Bonds are essentially loans you give to companies or governments, which pay you back with interest over a specified period. They're generally less risky than stocks because they promise regular interest payments and return of your initial investment at maturity. If you're someone who prefers stability over wild swings, bonds could be your go-to!

Mutual funds are like mixed flower beds where you combine several types of plants to spread out the risk. They track a collection of various stocks or bonds, offering diversification. This approach is perfect for beginners because it provides exposure to a wide range of assets, reducing the impact of poor performance from any single investment.

Here's how to start:

- Begin by researching different stocks, bonds and/or mutual funds.
- Open an investment account through a brokerage platform, many of which allow you to start with a minimal amount.
- Start investing gradually. Even small, regular contributions can grow significantly over time due to compound interest.

Setting clear investment goals and knowing your time horizon is also crucial. Are you saving for college tuition in two years, or are you building a retirement fund for 40 years down the line? Your goals will shape your strategy. Short-term goals might mean leaning towards safer investments like bonds. Long-term goals, on the other hand, allow you to ride out the ups and downs of the stock market for potentially higher gains.

In today's digital age, robo-advisors and investment apps are like having a pocketful of gardening tools. They make investing easy and accessible, especially for those who are tech-savvy. Robo-advisors use algorithms to manage your investments based on your risk tolerance and goals. Here's what to keep in mind when using them:

- Research different platforms. Popular ones include Betterment, Wealthfront, and Acorns.
- Input your financial goals and risk preferences. The robo-advisor will create a personalized portfolio for you.
- Monitor your investments periodically. While robo-advisors automate much of the process, it's good to stay informed about your portfolio's performance.

Investment apps can also offer educational tools and resources to help you learn as you grow your wealth. Some apps, like Acorns or Chime, even let you invest spare change from your everyday purchases, making it effortless to start small and build up over time.

Let's wrap things up with a few key takeaways: First, understand the risk levels of different investments. Stocks can offer high rewards but carry significant risks, whereas bonds provide more stability with smaller, modest returns. Second, consider starting with diversified, low-cost index funds or ETFs to spread out your risk. And finally, don't shy away from leveraging technology with robo-advisors and investment apps to make investing more accessible and manageable.

Investing isn't just about making money; it's about growing your financial literacy and securing your future. Like tending a garden, it requires patience, care, and sometimes a bit of trial and error. But with each step you take, you'll be nurturing your financial landscape to flourish for years to come.

Importance of Diversification

When you think about the world of investments, it might seem like a vast, confusing ocean. But don't worry, diving into this ocean can be an exciting journey if we take it step by step. So, let's start talking about why diversification are crucial for making smart financial decisions.

Diversification, like we said earlier, is all about spreading your investments and therefore, your risk, across different asset classes and industries. When you diversify, you spread your money across different investments, reducing the risk of losing everything if one sector takes a hit.

Consider this: If you put all your savings into tech stocks and the tech industry suddenly faces a downturn, you would find yourself in trouble. But if some of that money was also invested in real estate, consumer goods, or bonds, the impact would be less severe. Diversification doesn't guarantee profits, but it certainly mitigates losses.

Investing in Index Funds

While some people love the thrill of hand-picking individual stocks, there's a more reliable, less risky option that even seasoned investors swear by - Index Funds.

For example, an S&P 500 index fund is a type of investment fund that tracks the performance of the S&P 500, an index made up of 500 of the largest publicly traded companies in the U.S. These companies span various sectors, from tech giants like Apple to financial leaders like JPMorgan Chase. By investing in an S&P 500 index fund, you're essentially buying a small piece of all these companies at once.

While investing in individual stocks can sometimes deliver higher short-term gains, it's also riskier and requires more attention. For most investors, especially those looking for long-term growth with less risk, S&P 500 index funds offer a smarter, more reliable path to wealth.

Here's why some people consider investing in an S&P 500 index fund is often better than investing in individual stocks:

- Instant Diversification: Picking individual stocks can leave you vulnerable to the performance of just a few companies. If one stock tanks, your portfolio could take a big hit. With an S&P 500 index fund, you're investing in a broad range of companies across different sectors, reducing the risk associated with any single stock's performance.

- No Need for Constant Monitoring: Investing in individual stocks often requires constant research and monitoring to make sure you're not caught off guard by a sudden downturn in a company's performance. With an S&P 500 index fund, the fund automatically tracks the market, so you don't need to spend time analyzing financial reports or adjusting your portfolio frequently.

- Proven Long-Term Growth: Historically, the S&P 500 has delivered consistent returns, averaging around 7% to

10% annually over the long term (adjusted for inflation). Sure, some individual stocks can have higher highs, but they also come with much lower lows. By sticking with an S&P 500 index fund, you're likely to enjoy steady, long-term growth without the wild fluctuations.

Market Volatility: Staying Invested During Fluctuations

Markets don't move in straight lines. They go up, down, and sometimes sideways. This is called market volatility. It's like being on a roller coaster – which can be thrilling and also nerve-wracking. However, understanding this can help you stay calm and committed to your investment strategy.

When markets plummet, your instincts might tell you to sell off investments to cut losses. This is panic selling at the worst possible time. Data shows that staying invested through market dips allows portfolios to recover and grow over the long run. For instance, during the 2008 Global Financial Crisis, many who sold their investments faced significant losses. Those who stayed invested saw their portfolios bounce back and flourish as markets recovered.

There is a practical way to keep investing even when markets are fluctuating: dollar-cost averaging. This is a simple investing strategy where you invest the same amount of money regularly, no matter what the market is doing. Instead of trying to time the market, you buy more shares when prices are low and fewer shares when prices are high, which can help reduce the impact of market volatility over time.

Here is what you can do in order to achieve the goal:

- Set aside a fixed amount of money to invest regularly, regardless of market conditions.
- Spread your investments across various assets to maintain diversification.
- Avoid trying to time the market; consistency is the key.
- Keep emotions in check and follow your plan rigorously.

By investing consistently, you buy more shares when prices are low and fewer when they're high. Over time, this averages out the cost per share, and could lower your overall investment cost.

For example, if you decide to invest $100 every month, you will continue doing so whether the market is up or down. In January, the stock costs $10, so you buy 10 shares. In February, the price drops to $5, so you buy 20 shares. In March, the price goes up to $20, so you buy 5 shares. Over time, this strategy can help you build wealth while smoothing out the highs and lows of the market.

Introduction to Cryptocurrency

The Basics, Pros, and Cons

Now let's dive into something that's been all the buzz lately—cryptocurrency. You might have heard about Bitcoin, Ethereum, or even Dogecoin. And while this is not meant to be a complete guide to everything crypto, we're going to get into what exactly is cryptocurrency, and the pros and cons of making it a part of your overall investment strategy. Let's break it down in simple terms.

What is Cryptocurrency?

Cryptocurrency is a type of digital or virtual currency that uses cryptography for security. Unlike traditional currencies issued by governments (like the US dollar or the Euro), cryptocurrencies operate on technology called blockchain. A blockchain is a decentralized system spread across many computers that records all transactions made with a particular cryptocurrency. Think of it as a giant, transparent ledger that everyone can see but no one can alter.

Investing in cryptocurrency involves buying and holding digital currencies with the hope that their value will increase over time. Here's a basic rundown of how you can start:

- Choose a reliable exchange: You'll need to use a cryptocurrency exchange to buy and sell digital currencies. Some well-known exchanges include Coinbase, Binance, and Kraken. The Robinhood app also provides for an easy way to buy and sell digital assets.
- Create a digital wallet: This is where you store your cryptocurrencies. There are different types of wallets, including hardware wallets (physical devices) and software wallets (apps).
- Do your research: Cryptocurrencies are highly volatile. Before investing, learn about the specific cryptocurrency, its use case, and the team behind it.
- Start small: Given the high volatility, it's wise to start with a small investment and gradually increase it as you become more comfortable.

One of the most appealing aspects of cryptocurrency is the potential for high returns. For example, Bitcoin's value has skyrocketed from a few cents to tens of thousands of dollars over the past decade. This potential for significant gains attracts many young investors looking to grow their wealth rapidly. Additionally, cryptocurrencies offer accessibility; you don't need a large amount of money to start investing. You can buy fractions of a coin, making it possible to get started with even a small budget. The decentralized nature of cryptocurrencies also means they are not controlled by any single entity, such as a government or bank. This can offer a sense of security and autonomy for some investors, as it protects against government interference and manipulation.

However, investing in cryptocurrencies comes with its share of risks. The most notable is high volatility. Cryptocurrencies can experience extreme price fluctuations; what might be worth a lot today can plummet tomorrow. This makes them a risky investment, especially for those who cannot afford to lose their money. Another significant downside is the lack of regulation in the crypto market. Unlike traditional financial systems, the cryptocurrency market is still relatively unregulated, which can lead to scams and fraud. It's essential to be cautious and do thorough research before investing. Security risks are another concern. While blockchain technology is secure, the platforms and exchanges where you buy and store your crypto can be vulnerable to hacks. There have been numerous instances of exchanges being hacked, resulting in significant financial losses for investors.

Now, investing in cryptocurrency isn't all excitement and profit; there are significant pitfalls that young investors should be aware of.

Market manipulation is also a common issue in the crypto world. Large holders of a particular cryptocurrency, known as "whales," can cause massive price swings by buying or selling large quantities or sometimes even by just releasing a tweet about a certain cryptocurrency. This manipulation can lead to substantial financial losses for smaller investors. Scams and frauds are also rampant in the crypto space. From fake Initial Coin Offerings (ICOs) to phishing schemes, investors must be vigilant. Always double-check the legitimacy of the platform or the coin before investing. Regulatory changes can also impact the value and legality of cryptocurrencies. For example, China's crackdown on crypto mining and trading caused significant disruptions in the market. Technology risks are another concern. Cryptocurrencies rely on technology, and like any technology, they can have bugs or be subject to cyber attacks. For instance, Mt. Gox, a bitcoin exchange in Japan, was reportedly hacked several times in 2014, and over $450 million worth of Bitcoin was stolen. In 2024 money, at today's prices, that's over $58 billion – gone, as a result of a series of cyber attacks.

To navigate these risks, it's essential to use reputable exchanges and enable two-factor authentication (2FA) to protect your accounts. Storing your crypto in secure wallets, preferably hardware wallets for large amounts, can also help protect against hacks. Staying updated on the latest news and trends in the cryptocurrency world is crucial. Follow reliable sources and join reputable communities to stay informed. This continuous learning process helps you make better investment decisions and avoid potential pitfalls.

Investing in Bitcoin ETFs

If you've been keeping an eye on the cryptocurrency market, you've likely heard about the rise of Bitcoin. While buying Bitcoin directly has been the popular route for many investors, there's another option that's gaining attention - Bitcoin ETFs (Exchange-Traded Funds). A Bitcoin ETF is an investment fund that tracks the value of Bitcoin and trades on traditional stock exchanges like any other ETF. Instead of owning Bitcoin directly, you own shares of a fund that mirrors Bitcoin's performance. This allows you to get exposure to Bitcoin without having to buy and store the actual cryptocurrency. Bitcoin ETFs offer a simpler, safer and more regulated way to get into cryptocurrency.

Here's why investing in Bitcoin ETFs might be a better choice compared to buying Bitcoin directly:

- Easier to Invest: Buying Bitcoin directly can be tricky for beginners. Instead of navigating within a cryptocurrency exchange, you can invest in Bitcoin ETFs through traditional brokerage accounts, making it far more accessible and less confusing.

- Regulation and Security: Bitcoin ETFs are regulated by financial authorities, whereas the cryptocurrency market itself is still largely unregulated. By investing in an ETF, you're benefiting from the oversight of established financial systems that help protect investors from fraud and other risks associated with the crypto space.

- Tax Simplicity: Cryptocurrencies are subject to complex tax rules, and reporting gains or losses can be confusing.

Bitcoin ETFs, on the other hand, are taxed like any other stock or ETF, making tax reporting much simpler for investors.

- Easier to Sell: Selling Bitcoin directly can take time, especially during high-volume trading periods when exchanges get overloaded. With Bitcoin ETFs, you can trade just like any stock - buy and sell whenever the market is open, ensuring better liquidity and ease of transaction.

Cryptocurrency is an exciting new frontier in the world of investing and potentially a lucrative investment, but it comes with significant risks. By starting small, diversifying your investments, and staying informed, you can navigate the world of crypto more safely. Remember, it's essential to balance potential high rewards with the understanding of high risks and only you can decide if it's right for you and your individual financial situation. Yes, it offers the potential for high returns but comes with significant risks and uncertainties so it's not the right investment for everyone. With cryptocurrency, you should only invest what you can afford to lose. By understanding the basics, weighing the pros and cons, and taking steps to protect yourself, you can explore this digital currency world responsibly.

Taking the First Step With Investing

How do you get started with investing? A crucial first step is setting aside a portion of your income specifically for investments. Whether it's from a part-time job, allowance, or any side hustle, discipline yourself to save regularly. Initially, it might seem like a small amount, but over time, these contributions add up.

Consider investing using the 52 Week Rule – Invest $1 in week one, then $2 in week two, $3 in week three and so on, and you will have invested a total of $1,378 over the course of a year!

Now, this isn't just theory. Many successful investors began their journeys early. Take Warren Buffett, for example. He bought his first stock at age 11, and today he's one of the richest people in the world. Or consider someone closer to your generation: Farrah Gray, who became a millionaire at 14 through smart investments. The lesson here is clear – the earlier you start, the better your chances of reaping significant benefits in the long run.

Here is what you can do to set aside a portion of your income for investing:

- Begin by determining how much you can comfortably set aside each week or month from your earnings.
- Set up automatic transfers from your checking account to your investment account to ensure you are consistently setting aside funds without having to think about it each time.
- Start small, perhaps saving the equivalent of one hour's wage per day you work. This guideline makes it easier to manage while still being effective.
- Track your progress and adjust your investment goals as your income grows.

Next, educating yourself on investment options is key. There are numerous resources available – books, online courses, videos, blogs, and even apps that simulate real investing scenarios without using real money. These tools can teach you about different types of investments, such as stocks, bonds, mutual funds, and ETFs. You don't always have to follow the "pros". Do your own research. To educate yourself on investment options:

- Begin by exploring free educational websites and online courses that offer beginner-friendly content.
- Use investment simulations or games to practice investing in a risk-free environment.
- Follow financial news and read articles on various investment strategies and market trends.
- Consider joining forums or communities where members share insights and experiences about investing.

It's essential to take proactive steps towards financial independence. It's not just about hoping your investments will grow; it's about making informed decisions and actively managing your investment portfolio.

Engagement with real-life examples helps too. If you like Apple products, you may want to invest in Apple stock. Love Starbucks coffee? Why not own a piece of the company by buying a few shares! Following a company you know can make the process more relatable. Over time, you'll learn to diversify your investments, spreading your money across different companies and sectors to reduce risk.

Let's take the examples of Tommy and Elena. Tommy invested a portion of his summer earnings in an S&P 500 index fund at 18, while Elena waited to begin investing until she was 28. Tommy doesn't just end up with more money – he also has more experience and confidence navigating the unpredictable waters of the stock market as he grows older.

Another great thing about starting young is learning from your mistakes when the stakes are relatively low. You may experience ups and downs in the market, but these early lessons will prepare you for more significant investments later on. You'll understand how to research potential opportunities, balance risks, and remain patient for long-term gains.

Investing isn't something reserved for adults. It's a valuable skill you can begin developing right now. Think of it as a journey towards financial independence and security.

Is investing for everyone? No. You should not begin investing until you are relatively debt-free. The interest on debt, like credit cards or loans, can cost you more than what you would make from investments. If you are paying high interest rates, like 15% or more, it's hard to find any investment that gives you that kind of return on your money. By focusing on paying off your debt first, you'll save money and free yourself from those extra payments. Once you're debt-free, you'll have more money to invest and be in a better position to grow your wealth without worrying about interest piling up.

Remember, the main takeaways here are simple:

- Start investing early to take advantage of compound interest but wait until you are relatively debt-free.
- Allocate a portion of your income specifically for investments.
- Educate yourself on various investment options and keep learning.

- Take proactive steps to manage your finances and investments with a long-term perspective.

Summary

Building a Strong Financial Future

We've covered quite a bit about how to dive into the world of investments and financial growth. We've talked about compound interest, different types of investment vehicles like stocks, bonds, and mutual funds, the importance of diversification, and strategies like dollar-cost averaging. We've also emphasized starting early and using technology to help manage investments. It's all about setting yourself on a path toward financial stability.

Remember when we first mentioned that starting early gives you a massive advantage? It's worth revisiting this point because it's the cornerstone of everything we've discussed. The sooner you plant your financial seeds, the taller and sturdier your money tree will grow. Warren Buffet started young, and you can too. There's no magic trick - just the consistent application of simple principles. While it might seem like a difficult task, the consequences of not starting early are pretty significant. Waiting too long means missing out on valuable time for your money to grow due to compound interest.

So where do we stand now? Hopefully, you're feeling a bit more comfortable with these concepts and see how they fit together to build your financial future. You might still have concerns about market volatility or picking the right investments. That's totally normal. The key is not to get overwhelmed. Take baby steps and learn as you go. Every successful investor started where you are now, questioning and learning.

On a broader scale, early investing doesn't just impact your personal wealth. It contributes to your overall financial literacy, making you a more informed citizen capable of making better economic decisions. This knowledge can even spill over into other areas of your life, like understanding credit, loans, and even how businesses operate.

And finally, consider this: What kind of financial future do you want? Picture yourself 10, 20, or even 40 years down the line. The decisions you make today will shape that future.

Start small but start now! Open that investment account, read up on different investment options, and invest consistently. Who knows - you might become the next Warren Buffet or Farrah Gray!

CHAPTER 6

NAVIGATING TAXES AND INCOME MANAGEMENT

Managing money can be tricky, especially when you're just starting out. Think back to your first paycheck—exciting, right? But then you glance at the numbers and notice the deductions, taxes, and other terms that seem so confusing. What do you really end up with after all those subtractions, and how should you manage that amount wisely? Understanding these mysteries isn't just for accountants or financial gurus; it's crucial for anyone looking to navigate the adult world smoothly.

Let's say you've landed a part-time job. You expect to pocket all your hard-earned cash, but instead, there's this whole chunk missing for taxes. Where does it go? What's a "deduction" and a "credit?" Why are they important? Understanding deductions can help you reduce your taxable income, making sure you're not paying more taxes than you need to. Tax credits are even better because they directly cut down the tax you owe. And then there's filing your tax return—a task that sounds intimidating but is essentially a summary report you send to the government of your earnings and expenses.

In this chapter, we'll guide you through managing taxes and your income. You'll learn how to calculate your take-home pay and create a budget that works for you. We'll break down essential concepts like tax deductions and credits, showing you how to leverage them to keep more money in your pocket. By understanding these vital components, you'll not only stay on good terms with the tax authorities but also lay the foundation for a secure financial future. So, buckle up, grab a calculator, and get ready to demystify the world of taxes and income management.

Calculating Take-Home Pay

Calculating your take-home pay is key to managing your finances. Understanding the deductions and taxes that reduce your gross income will help you plan your spending, saving, and budgeting more effectively.

First, let's break down what calculating take-home pay involves. It's simply subtracting taxes and other deductions from your gross income. Think of your paycheck like an iceberg: what you see above the water is your net pay – the amount you take home. But lurking below are all the deductions.

Understanding the breakdown of a paycheck is crucial for managing your finances and knowing where your money goes. Here's a detailed look at the common components and deductions you might find on a typical paycheck:

Gross Pay

This is your total earnings before any deductions. It includes:

- Regular Pay: Your base salary or hourly wage multiplied by the number of hours worked.

- Overtime Pay: Additional pay for hours worked beyond the regular work schedule, typically at a higher rate.

- Bonuses/Commissions: Extra earnings based on performance or sales.

Deductions

Deductions are amounts taken out of your gross pay for various reasons. They can be categorized into mandatory and voluntary deductions.

Mandatory Deductions are those required by law and include:

- Federal Income Tax: This is based on your income level and the information you provided on your W-4 form (filing status, number of allowances, etc.). It's withheld to go towards your federal income taxes.

- State Income Tax: Not all states have this, but if yours does, a percentage of your income goes towards state taxes. Some urban areas like New York City, Philadelphia, Detroit, Columbus, St. Louis, and Portland even have a local income tax that is withheld from paychecks for those working and/or living in the cities that impose them, similar to federal and state income taxes.

- Social Security Tax: A federal tax that funds Social Security benefits, which are paid to retirees and disabled individuals. The rate is currently 6.2% of your gross pay.

- Medicare Tax: A federal tax that funds Medicare, providing health insurance for people 65 and older and certain younger people with disabilities. The rate is 1.45% of your gross pay.

Voluntary Deductions are optional and based on your personal choices. They include:

- Health Insurance Premiums: If you have health insurance through your employer, your share of the premiums will be deducted from your paycheck.
- Retirement Contributions: Money you choose to contribute to a retirement plan like a 401(k) or 403(b). Often, employers will match a portion of your contributions. If they do, take advantage of that free money!
- Life and Disability Insurance: Premiums for additional insurance policies provided through your employer.
- Flexible Spending Account (FSA) or Health Savings Account (HSA) Contributions: Pre-tax contributions to accounts used to pay for medical expenses.
- Union Dues: If you're a member of a union, dues will be deducted from your pay.

Net Pay

Your Net Pay is also called your "take-home pay." This is the amount you receive after all deductions are subtracted from your gross pay. It's the actual amount deposited into your bank account or received via check. Let's assume a bi-weekly paycheck for an employee with a gross pay of $2,000:

GROSS PAY	$2000.00
- FEDERAL INCOME TAX	200.00
- STATE INCOME TAX	100.00
- SOCIAL SECURITY TAX (6.2%)	124.00
- MEDICARE TAX (1.45%)	29.00
- HEALTH INSURANCE PREMIUM	75.00
- 401(k) CONTRIBUTION	100.00
= NET PAY	$1,372.00

Understanding each component of your paycheck helps you manage your finances more effectively, ensuring you're aware of where your earnings go and how much you have available to spend or save.

Federal, state and local taxes withheld from your pay fund essential public services like police, firefighters, sanitation, and infrastructure, including education, transportation, public safety, and healthcare. These taxes fund programs that benefit society as a whole, providing support for those in need and contributing to the overall well-being and progress of the country. Social Security and Medicare, also known as FICA taxes, ensure that there's a safety net for others now and for you when you're older or if you become disabled. While it may feel frustrating to see these amounts taken from your earnings, remember that they serve important social functions.

Managing your paycheck isn't just about knowing where your money goes. It's about wisely dividing it between essential expenses and savings. Think of it as laying the foundation for a secure financial future. Here are some tips to guide you:

- Set aside money for fixed expenses first. This includes rent or mortgage payments, utilities, groceries, and any installment loans you might have.
- After covering your essential needs, direct some funds towards savings. Aim to save at least 20% of your income. If that's not feasible now, start small and work your way up.
- Keep track of discretionary spending. Whether it's eating out, new clothes, or entertainment, make sure you don't blow your budget on non-essential items.
- Create an emergency fund. Life happens, and having three to six months' worth of expenses set aside can make unexpected situations less stressful.

Using online tools or worksheets can simplify the process of paycheck calculations. Many websites and apps let you input your gross pay, then they calculate and subtract deductions, and give you an estimate of your take-home pay. They require you to enter details about your earnings, withholding status, and additional deductions and can generate an instant breakdown of your net pay, making it easier to understand where each portion of your salary is going.

Mobile apps often come with features that allow you to track your spending and savings goals over time, providing a comprehensive picture of your financial health.

To recap, knowing how to calculate your take-home pay is more than just a math exercise. It's a tool to help you create realistic budgets and set achievable financial goals. You can plan for your dreams, whether that's traveling, buying a car, or simply having the peace of mind that comes with financial security.

By understanding every detail of your paycheck, from federal and state taxes to Social Security contributions and voluntary benefits, you gain insight into how much you really earn. Effective paycheck management ensures that your hard-earned money works for you, covering necessary expenses while allowing room for savings and discretionary spending. Utilizing online tools takes the guesswork out of the equation, enabling you to focus on enjoying the fruits of your labor.

Overall, it's about striking a balance between economic growth and human welfare. When you're informed and proactive about your take-home pay, you put yourself in a powerful position to make choices that benefit not just your wallet but your overall well-being.

Understanding Common Tax Terms

Understanding common tax terms and their impact on personal finance can save you from many future headaches. Let's break it down, one term at a time.

First, there are several types of income. There's earned income – the money you have made in salary, wages or tips from working at a job or the profit from running a business. Unearned income is income you earn passively – without performing any work, like interest or dividend income you earn from savings accounts or investments. Capital gains income is when you sell an asset, such as a stock, for more than you bought it.

When we talk about deductions, we're referring to certain expenses that can be subtracted from your total income to reduce the taxable portion. Think of it like getting a discount on your taxes for specific things you spend money on. For example, if you're paying interest on a student loan or have medical expenses above a certain threshold, these can sometimes count as deductions. Even simple things like contributing to an IRA – an Individual Retirement Account - may also qualify.

Deductions are helpful because they reduce the amount of income that's taxed. Standard and itemized deductions are essential components of a tax return that help reduce your taxable income, potentially lowering the amount of taxes you owe. The standard deduction is a fixed dollar amount set by the IRS that taxpayers can deduct from their income without the need to itemize specific expenses. This amount varies depending on your filing status (single, married filing jointly, etc.) and is adjusted annually for inflation. It has also significantly increased in recent years due to tax law changes.

On the other hand, itemized deductions allow taxpayers to deduct certain eligible expenses, such as mortgage interest, state and local taxes, medical expenses, and charitable contributions, but require detailed documentation.

You should calculate your expenses that would qualify to be itemized deductions before filing your tax return. If they are more than the standard deduction, take the itemized deduction. If not, go with the standard deduction.

Most people opt for the standard deduction because it simplifies the tax filing process but more importantly, their itemized deductions are less than the standard deduction the government gives you. Therefore, using the standard results in a higher deduction amount than they would receive by itemizing. This choice not only saves time but also reduces the complexity and potential for errors in their tax return. So, deductions lower your overall tax by allowing you to subtract certain eligible expenses from your total income.

Now, tax credits. This is where things get a lot more impactful. A tax credit directly reduces the amount of tax you owe, dollar for dollar. Unlike deductions that reduce your taxable income, credits cut straight to the chase—they lower your actual tax bill. If you've ever heard of the Child Tax Credit or the Earned Income Tax Credit, those are examples of these powerful tax credits.

For instance, let's say you owe $1,500 in taxes but qualify for a tax credit worth $1,000. Your tax bill would then drop to just $500, saving you a significant chunk of change. There are different types of tax credits too: refundable and nonrefundable. Refundable credits are great; if they bring your tax bill below zero, you can get a refund for the difference. Nonrefundable credits, on the other hand, can only reduce your tax liability to zero but can't earn you a refund beyond that point.

Take the American Opportunity Tax Credit, aimed at easing the burden of college costs. This credit can offer up to $2,500 per eligible student for qualified education expenses. It's partially refundable, meaning if the credit reduces your tax to zero, you could receive a portion of any remaining amount of the credit, up to $1,000, as a refund. That's not just beneficial to your wallet; it's a meaningful financial boost when you need it the most.

Now, let's turn our attention to tax returns. These documents are filed with the government to report your income and determine your tax obligations, due by April 15th of the following year. Filing a tax return might sound intimidating, but think of it as filling out a financial summary report. You gather all your important forms, like W-2s and 1099s, which detail your earnings from work, savings or investments, and include a summary of any taxes already paid. You figure out what you can deduct from your income. Then you tally everything up to see whether you owe additional taxes or get a refund.

When you look at a tax return, it can feel overwhelming with the many lines and various forms involved. However, it can be simplified into a basic formula that explains how your tax liability is calculated. At its core, it all comes down to determining your taxable income and applying the correct tax rate, while accounting for any deductions and tax credits along the way.

Tax returns have many more details, but this chart breaks down the key steps: starting with your income, subtracting deductions to get taxable income, applying the tax rate to find your tax amount, and finally subtracting any tax credits to determine your total tax liability.

INCOME
- DEDUCTIONS
= TAXABLE INCOME
x TAX RATE
= TAX
- TAX CREDITS
= TAX LIABILITY

You might be wondering why this matters. Well, understanding your tax return helps you make informed decisions about your finances. When you know what goes into your return, you can better plan throughout the year—adjusting your withholding, making estimated payments, or even saving receipts for deductible expenses. Plus, filing accurately and on time keeps you in good standing with Uncle Sam and avoids potential penalties or interest.

Bringing it all together, understanding these terms—income, deductions, credits, and tax returns—is crucial for making smart financial choices. With a clearer picture of how each element influences your tax situation, you're better equipped to manage your money, ensure compliance with tax regulations, and maximize your savings.

So, what's the key takeaway from all this? Familiarity with tax terms like deductions, credits, and tax returns can empower you to plan better financially. It's not just about keeping more of your hard-earned money; it's about staying informed and compliant with tax laws. By grasping these concepts, you gain control over your financial destiny, enabling you to navigate the often complex world of taxes with confidence.

Ultimately, taxes are more than just numbers on a form; they're integral to your broader financial health. Informed tax management isn't just for accountants—it's a critical skill for everyone. From ensuring you get the most out of deductions and credits to filing accurate returns, every bit of knowledge helps. So take a deep breath, arm yourself with information, and tackle those taxes head-on!

Understanding some of these basic tax principles early on can set you up for success and maybe even save you from some major stress down the road. Remember, the goal isn't to become a tax expert overnight but to equip yourself with essential knowledge so you can make informed decisions and protect your financial health.

Other Taxes You May Encounter

In addition to the income taxes deducted from your paycheck, there's another tax you may typically pay: sales tax. Sales taxes are applied to everyday purchases and serve as a crucial source of revenue for state and local governments. Whenever you buy items like clothes, electronics, or even a snack, a percentage of the total cost is added as sales tax. This revenue helps fund essential services such as public schools, roads, parks, and emergency services that everyone relies on. By paying sales tax, you contribute to maintaining and improving your community's infrastructure and public services, benefiting both you and those around you. Understanding sales tax can also help you budget more effectively and be aware of the true cost of the items you buy.

As you get older, you'll encounter various other types of taxes beyond just income and sales taxes.

There are property taxes, which homeowners pay based on their home's value, helping fund local services like public schools, police, and fire departments. Another common tax is the self-employment tax, which is a combination of Social Security and Medicare taxes that self-employed individuals must pay on their earnings so that they may collect Social Security benefits and qualify for Medicare in the future.

Some items like gasoline, cigarettes, firearms, alcohol, automobiles, or airline tickets, have excise taxes. These taxes are often included in the price of the product and are typically levied on goods considered harmful or non-essential. Certain vehicles, especially those that are heavy or not fuel-efficient, may have excise taxes. This can include trucks and luxury cars. When you purchase a plane ticket, a portion of the cost goes to excise taxes, which fund airport and airway improvements. Excise taxes on firearms and ammunition help fund wildlife conservation and maintain shooting ranges. In recent years, some localities have started to impose excise taxes on sugary drinks to discourage excessive consumption and promote developing healthy habits.

You'll also encounter capital gains taxes if you invest in stocks or real estate and sell them for a profit. Capital gains taxes are a type of tax you pay on the profit you make from selling an asset, like stocks, bonds, or real estate. Let's say you bought a video game for $20 and later sold it to a friend for $30. The $10 profit you made is similar to a capital gain. When it comes to investments, if you buy a stock for $100 and sell it later for $150, you have a $50 capital gain. The government requires you to pay taxes on that $50 profit, which is the capital gains tax. The rate of this tax can vary depending on how long you held the investment before selling it. If you held it for more than a year, you might pay a lower rate, called the long-term capital gains tax. If you held it for a year or less, you would pay a higher rate, called the short-term capital gains tax. Understanding capital gains taxes is important because it helps you plan your investments and know how much of your profit you'll keep after taxes.

Understanding all these different types of taxes is important because it helps you manage your finances better and prepare for the responsibilities that come with adulthood.

Strategies for Effective Income Management and Budgeting

Alright, let's dive into some practical ways to handle your income and budget effectively. We're all navigating the same sea of uncertainties, but having a solid game plan can make things smoother.

As we've said before, tracking your expenses is like keeping a diary but for your money. It's not exciting, but it's crucial. Managing your finances without tracking expenses feels like you're sailing a boat without a navigation system. You'll end up somewhere, but it might not be where you want to go.

By jotting down every single expense (yes, even that $1 candy bar), you'll be able to categorize them and help identify patterns. At the end of each week, review your list. Look for areas where you're spending more than you realized.

You're likely to spot places where you could save by examining where your money goes. Maybe those daily lattes are costing more than you thought, or perhaps there's a subscription service you rarely use. You might even find a few that you've never used, yet you pay for them each month. Cutting back even slightly in these areas can free up cash for other needs or savings.

Next, set financial goals based on your income. We have to be realistic when it comes to setting financial goals based on the money we have coming in. Think of this as plotting your course on a map. You don't just wander around aimlessly; you set a destination and figure out how to get there. But you also don't unrealistically decide one day you're going to take a walk across the country. Financially speaking, it's the same deal. Setting clear, realistic goals helps steer your funds in the right direction.

To break this down:

- Determine your short-term goals (like saving for a new phone) and long-term goals (like college tuition).
- Prioritize these goals. Which ones are non-negotiable, and which can wait?
- Allocate your income with these priorities in mind. If your goal is to save $500 for a trip next summer, work out how much you need to set aside monthly to reach that target.

Remember, it's about knowing your big picture and taking baby steps towards it. Avoid splurging on items that don't align with your goals. This kind of strategy ensures that your hard-earned money is working for you and not against you.

Now let's talk about implementing budgeting techniques like the 50/30/20 rule we discussed earlier. This method suggests dividing your income into three buckets: needs, wants, and savings. Here's how it works:

- 50% of your income should cover needs like rent, groceries, utilities, and transportation.

- 30% goes towards wants, including eating out, entertainment, and hobbies.
- 20% should be allocated to savings or debt repayment.

Putting this into practice is easy. First, calculate your monthly net income after taxes. Let's say it's $2,000. Now, based on the 50/30/20 rule, allocate $1,000 for your needs, $600 for your wants, and $400 for savings or paying off debt.

The beauty of this system is its flexibility; it gives you a clear framework while allowing room for personal adjustments. For instance, if your rent takes up more than 50% of your income, you may need to cut down on wants or save more aggressively to balance out your budget.

Finally, regularly reviewing and adjusting your budget is key to staying afloat financially. Life is unpredictable, and so is our spending and income. Whether you've received a raise, taken on extra expenses, or had a change in lifestyle, revisiting your budget ensures it remains aligned with your current situation.

Here's how you can keep your budget in check:

- At the end of each month, compare your actual spending with your budgeted amounts. Are you consistently overspending in one category? Adjustments may be needed.
- If you find a surplus in any category, consider transferring it to your savings or investing it.

- When unexpected expenses come up, reallocate funds from different categories rather than pulling out the credit card impulsively, which could lead to debt.

Regularly tweaking your budget reflects changing circumstances and keeps you prepared for future financial needs. It's like course-correcting your journey when encountering an unexpected storm.

In essence, developing sound budgeting habits is all about enhancing financial stability and paving the path toward long-term wealth accumulation. It might feel tedious at first, but mastering it brings peace of mind and control over your financial destiny.

No one said adulting was easy, but having these strategies in place can make it a lot less challenging. Everyone's financial journey is different—what works for someone else might not work for you. It's okay to try, fail, and readjust. The most important thing is that you're taking steps towards understanding and managing your finances better. After all, it's your journey, and you've got the helm.

The Role of Taxes in Financial Planning

Let's dive into taxes and how they play a role in our financial planning and savings. Taxes might sound boring or even intimidating, but understanding them can actually help you make smarter decisions with your money.

Taxes Impact Disposable Income

First things first, taxes have a direct impact on your disposable income, which is the amount of money you have left after paying your taxes. This disposable income is what you use to save, invest, or simply enjoy life. The key takeaway here is that higher taxes mean less money in your pocket to play around with. So, naturally, it affects your ability to save and invest.

Let's think of it like this; your paycheck is a pie. Taxes take one big slice of that pie right off the bat. The remaining pie is yours to distribute as you wish. Whether you're saving for college, buying that cool new gadget, or investing in stocks, all those actions depend on how big your remaining slice is.

Tax-Efficient Strategies

Now, let's talk about how you can keep more of that pie to yourself by using tax-efficient strategies—these are essentially smart ways to handle your money so you owe less in taxes. One popular strategy is contributing to retirement accounts like an IRA or a 401(k). These accounts often allow you to defer paying taxes until you withdraw the money, which can be years down the line. Another useful tool is educational savings plans, such as a 529 plan, which offers tax advantages specifically for education expenses.

You should always take advantage of employer-sponsored retirement plans like 401(k)s. These allow you to save some of your salary, on a pre-tax basis, towards your retirement. Pre-tax basis means that the money you put in the retirement is not taxed now but rather later when you begin to withdraw the money in your retirement years. And the interest or gains you earn every year are not taxed each year either – they grow tax-deferred – deferred until, again, you begin withdrawing the money. Thereby you're achieving two goals - lowering your income taxes now and saving for your retirement. Some employers even match your contributions up to a certain percentage, which is like free money.

If your employer does not offer any employer sponsored plans, you should explore Individual Retirement Accounts (IRAs). Traditional IRAs let you defer taxes much like 401(k) plans but there also are Roth IRAs. Roth IRAs give you no tax benefit now but offer you tax-free withdrawals in retirement.

Look into 529 plans if you're planning to save for college. Contributions grow tax-free, and withdrawals for educational purposes are also tax-free.

Consider Health Savings Accounts (HSAs) if you have high-deductible health insurance. Contributions are tax-deductible, and withdrawals for medical expenses are tax-free.

Implementing these strategies will not only help you save more but also ensure your investments grow in a tax-efficient manner.

Compliance with Tax Laws and Deadlines

No one enjoys dealing with penalties or additional interest charges because they missed a tax deadline. Ensuring compliance with tax laws and meeting deadlines is crucial for maintaining financial health. Penalties can quickly eat away at your savings, creating unnecessary stress and financial strain.

Here's what you can do to stay compliant:

- Keep track of important tax deadlines, such as when quarterly estimated taxes are due if you're self-employed.

- Maintain organized records of all your financial transactions. That means keeping receipts, careful investment records, and other documentation. If you're unsure, keep it! At tax time you can figure out what you need and don't need.

- Adjust your withholding allowances as needed throughout the year. If you have too little withheld, you'll owe a large sum at tax time. If you withhold too much, you'll get a large refund at tax time. And while you may think that's great, it's basically giving an interest-free loan to the government. They get the use of your money throughout the year.

- Use tax software or consult with a tax professional to make sure you're doing everything the right way and taking all possible deductions and credits.

By following these steps, you'll steer clear of common pitfalls and maintain a healthy financial standing.

Taxes as Part of Overall Financial Strategy

So we've covered how taxes affect disposable income and how to manage them efficiently, but there's a broader picture here. Viewing taxes as a part of your overall financial strategy can lead to better resource allocation and wealth preservation. Instead of seeing taxes as a burden, think of them as another factor to consider when making financial decisions.

For instance, in the future, if you're thinking about selling an investment like a stock or a real estate property or withdrawing money from your retirement account early, you should always also consider the tax implications. Sometimes holding onto an asset just a bit longer can significantly reduce your tax bill (long-term capital gains tax rate versus the short-term capital gain tax rate). If you need to access funds, some retirement plans allow you to take a loan out against your account assets instead of withdrawing the money. Similarly, making charitable donations can provide valuable tax deductions while also allowing you to support causes you care about. All it takes is a little extra research or asking the right people the right questions to see what your best options are.

Think of your finances as a jigsaw puzzle where each piece—income, spending, saving, investing, and taxes—fits together to create a complete picture. The goal is to optimize how each piece fits to achieve financial security and growth. Integrating tax considerations into your financial planning helps you preserve more wealth over time, enhancing your financial security and building a more robust financial future.

Integrating tax considerations into your financial planning isn't just wise—it's essential for enhancing financial security and wealth building. By understanding how taxes impact disposable income, using tax-efficient strategies, ensuring compliance with tax laws, and incorporating taxes into your overall financial strategy, you're setting yourself up for success.

Remember:

- Taxes affect your disposable income and, consequently, your ability to save and invest.

- Employing tax-efficient strategies can optimize your savings.
- Staying compliant with tax laws and deadlines avoids unnecessary penalties and maintains financial health.
- Thinking of taxes as part of your overall financial strategy can lead to better resource allocation and wealth preservation.

Armed with this knowledge, you're not just handling your finances wisely, you're mastering them. Taxes don't have to be a headache, they can be a useful tool in your financial toolkit. The next time you look at your paycheck or think about your savings, remember the importance of taxes in shaping your financial journey.

Summary

Integrating Tax Knowledge for Better Income Management

We've dived deep into the nitty-gritty of handling taxes, managing your paycheck, and budgeting wisely. These are crucial aspects of personal finance that can seem overwhelming at first but become much more manageable when broken down into simpler chunks.

We discussed calculating take-home pay, which is another cornerstone of money management. By grasping how much of your salary actually lands in your bank account after taxes and other deductions, you're better equipped to budget effectively. Think of it as mapping out your financial journey—it's essential to know where you stand before planning where you want to go.

Then we talked about other taxes and common tax terms like deductions, credits, and what filing a tax return involves. Understanding these basics is not just about getting through tax season without breaking a sweat; it's about setting yourself up for financial success. Knowing what deductions and credits you qualify for means you get to keep more of your hard-earned money.

Effective paycheck management isn't just about crunching numbers—it's a way to ensure stability and peace of mind. Allocating funds for fixed expenses, savings, discretionary spending, and an emergency fund prepares you for both daily needs and unexpected surprises. Utilizing online tools can make this process even smoother, offering instant insights into your financial health.

And finally, we explored income management and how it aligns with budgeting strategies. Whether it's tracking every single expense or using a system like the 50/30/20 rule, these techniques help you stay on top of your finances and work towards your goals. Budgeting might seem tedious initially, but it's incredibly rewarding once you see the benefits stacking up over time. Regularly reviewing and adjusting your budget keeps you flexible and prepared for life's curveballs.

So, what should concern you as a young adult stepping into financial independence? The main thing is to stay informed and proactive. Not knowing how taxes work, or how to manage your paycheck and budget effectively, can lead to unnecessary stress and financial pitfalls. But armed with the knowledge from this chapter, you're already ahead of the game.

On a broader scale, understanding these principles doesn't just benefit you personally—it contributes to a healthier economic environment. When individuals manage their finances well, they're less likely to fall into debt and more likely to contribute positively to the community and society at large.

Looking forward, remember that mastering money management skills is an ongoing journey. There's always more to learn and room to grow. Stay curious, keep educating yourself, and don't be afraid to ask questions. Financial literacy is a lifelong skill that will serve you well no matter where life takes you. Navigate your financial future with confidence.

CHAPTER 7

PREPARING FINANCIALLY FOR HIGHER EDUCATION

Do the costs of college—like tuition, books, and housing—feel overwhelming? What if we told you there's a way to make it all manageable, even without sinking into debt? It involves knowing your way around scholarships, grants, and loans.

Feeling lost when figuring out how to pay for college is completely normal. Many students don't realize the difference between "free money" like grants and scholarships, and loans that you'll eventually have to repay with interest. Take the examples of Khloe and John, for instance. Khloe knew she needed financial help but was drowning in confusion over where to start. Luckily, her high school counselor pointed her toward scholarship search engines and local community resources. So, she soon found herself applying for and receiving multiple scholarships tailored to her academic achievements and community involvement. On the flip side, John didn't seek advice early enough, relying heavily on loans, and now he's grappling with monthly repayments.

In this chapter, we'll explore college funding and break down different sources of financial aid, from need-based grants to merit-based scholarships and federal loans. You'll discover practical steps for researching and applying for these opportunities, and we'll touch on the importance of understanding loan terms to avoid long-term financial stress. By the end, you'll have a strategy for piecing together different funding sources to cover your college costs, like solving a puzzle. This knowledge will empower you to make informed decisions and ease some of those college cost jitters.

Exploring Various Sources of College Funding

Knowing the difference between grants, loans, and scholarships is key to making informed decisions about funding your education. Grants and scholarships are often referred to as "free money" because they don't need to be repaid, unlike loans which come with an obligation to pay back with interest. Grants are usually need-based, meaning they're awarded based on your financial situation. If your family earns below a certain amount, you may qualify for federal or state grants. Scholarships, on the other hand, are usually merit-based or tied to specific characteristics like academic achievements, extracurricular involvement, or even unique traits such as being part of a particular ethnicity or community.

Once you've got a handle on these differences, the next step is researching available grants and scholarships. It might seem overwhelming at first, but there are tons of resources available. Start by talking to your high school guidance counselor. They can provide guidance tailored to your circumstances. Online platforms like Scholarships.com, Fastweb or College Board also house massive databases of scholarships you can filter through based on your profile. Be sure to read eligibility criteria carefully and stick to application deadlines. Local community organizations, businesses, and of course, colleges themselves often offer scholarships, so don't overlook those opportunities.

Understanding loan options while being mindful of the implications of student debt is another critical layer. Federal loans should generally be your first choice because they tend to have lower interest rates and more flexible repayment options. The U.S. Department of Education offers Direct Subsidized Loans, which don't accrue interest while you're in school, and Direct Unsubsidized Loans that start accumulating interest right away. Consider private loans from banks or credit unions only after exhausting federal loan options, as they tend to have higher interest rates and stricter terms.

When thinking about loans, it's essential to understand the long-term impact. Borrowing more than you can realistically repay after graduation can cause financial stress. Aim to borrow only what you need to cover essential expenses - tuition, fees, books, and living costs - while trying to save money on non-essential items.

Strategizing a financial plan that combines different funding sources can significantly lighten the financial weight of college tuition. Think of it like assembling pieces of a puzzle. You've got grants, scholarships, federal loans, work-study programs, internships, and maybe even some savings or contributions from family. Combining these elements effectively requires a bit of planning but can ultimately pave the way for a smoother college experience financially.

Here's a streamlined approach to creating your financial plan:

- Map out your total college costs including tuition, room and board, books, and personal expenses.

- Determine how much free aid (grants and scholarships) you're eligible for.

- Calculate how much you'll realistically need to take out in loans, if any.

- Look into work-study or internship opportunities offered by your school to earn money while gaining valuable work experience.

- Set up a budget to track your spending and avoid unnecessary expenses and debts during your college years.

Exploring different college funding options gives you the freedom to make informed decisions that support your education without overwhelming debt. The key takeaway here is that a balanced approach—one that prioritizes grants and scholarships, understands loan implications, and strategizes intelligently—can set you on a path to achieving your educational goals with minimal financial strain.

It's crucial to keep your long-term goals in mind and stay open to adjusting your plans as new opportunities arise. The road to funding your college education doesn't have to be traveled alone. Leverage every resource available to you, keep an eye on deadlines, and don't hesitate to seek advice from mentors or counselors when needed. With a structured approach and a clear understanding of the different funding options, you'll be better equipped to navigate this significant phase of your life.

Moreover, being well-organized and proactive can immensely benefit you in the long run. Make a checklist of all your applications and start early. This gives you ample time to gather necessary documents, write compelling essays, and ensure every requirement is met. Be persistent and thorough in your research, as sometimes the best opportunities aren't the most obvious ones.

To summarize, the journey of financing your college education involves understanding the types of financial aid available, diligently researching those opportunities, comprehending the responsibilities tied to student loans, and crafting a comprehensive financial plan that minimizes debt and maximizes your educational prospects. It's not just about getting through college; it's about graduating with the least amount of financial baggage, ready to embark on your career with confidence and stability.

Arming yourself with knowledge will empower you to make choices that align with both your academic ambitions and financial realities. Start now, dig deep, and chart a course that leads not just to a degree, but to a future where financial pressures don't overshadow your achievements.

Tips for Researching and Applying for Financial Aid Programs

One of the most crucial steps in easing the burden of college expenses is understanding how to effectively research and apply for financial aid programs. This knowledge not only opens up a plethora of opportunities but also ensures that students can make informed decisions about their educational future.

Researching financial aid programs early in your high school career can significantly boost your chances of securing funds. Start as early as possible, as many scholarships and grants have specific deadlines and requirements. By beginning your search early, you create a roadmap of important dates and criteria that must be met.

Here are some steps to help you stay organized:

- Make a list of potential scholarships, grants, and other financial aid opportunities.
- Note down their application deadlines and requirements.
- Keep a calendar specifically for these deadlines so you don't miss an important date.
- Break down the tasks required for each application into smaller, manageable steps – such as do you need to supply them with a transcript, essay or letters of recommendations?

Starting early gives you time to gather documents, request recommendation letters, and write strong essays. This proactive approach avoids last-minute stress and allows you to submit well-prepared applications. Create a checklist of requirements for each financial assistance opportunity you're pursuing, along with taking note of the appropriate deadlines. Staying organized increases your chances of receiving aid.

Next, completing the Free Application for Federal Student Aid (FAFSA) accurately and promptly is another vital step. FAFSA serves as a gateway to federal financial aid, including grants, loans, and work-study opportunities. It opens doors to state and institutional aid programs as well.

To make the most out of FAFSA:

- Begin filling it out as soon as it becomes available on October 1st each year.
- Use the online version for a faster and easier experience.
- Gather all necessary information such as Social Security numbers, income tax returns, bank statements, and investment records before starting the application.
- Double-check every entry to ensure accuracy; even small errors can affect the amount of aid you receive.

The process might seem intimidating, but remember that there are numerous resources available to assist you, including online guides and school counselors. Setting aside enough time to complete FAFSA forms without rushing increases your chances of avoiding mistakes and securing the maximum amount of financial aid.

Don't underestimate the value of seeking guidance from school counselors or financial aid offices either. They offer a treasure trove of knowledge about available grants and scholarships tailored to your situation. Leveraging these support services can help you understand the steps needed to pay for your degree.

Engaging with these experts can provide you with:

- A clearer understanding of complex application processes.
- Access to insider tips on lesser-known scholarships and grants.
- Personalized advice based on your academic performance and financial situation.

- Assistance with appealing for additional aid if your financial circumstances change unexpectedly.

Remember that these professionals are there to help you. Don't hesitate to ask questions or seek clarification on anything that seems confusing. Their expertise can guide you through the maze of financial aid options and help you find the best fit for your needs.

In addition to professional guidance, understanding the importance of demonstrating both financial need and academic merit in your scholarship applications can greatly enhance your prospects. While financial need is determined by your family's financial situation, academic merit reflects your achievements, talents, and potential.

When crafting your scholarship applications:

- Explain how financial aid will alleviate any specific challenges you face.
- Highlight your academic successes, extracurricular activities, and leadership roles.
- Tailor your essays to reflect the values and goals of the scholarship you're applying for.
- Provide strong recommendation letters that speak to your character and accomplishments.

By showcasing both your financial need and academic excellence, you present a comprehensive picture of why you deserve the aid. This dual approach increases your appeal to scholarship committees looking for well-rounded candidates who can benefit the most from their financial support.

Ultimately, being proactive in researching and applying for financial aid programs can open up a world of opportunities. Not only does it help reduce the financial strain associated with higher education, but it also allows you to focus more on your studies and less on financial worries. As you navigate this journey, staying organized, seeking expert advice, and presenting yourself authentically will go a long way towards securing the resources you need to achieve your academic dreams.

Navigating the world of scholarships can seem overwhelming, but with a bit of guidance, the process becomes much more manageable. Start by identifying scholarship opportunities that align with your personal interests, community involvement, and academic achievements. This approach can significantly increase your likelihood of receiving awards. Here is what you can do to achieve this goal:

- List your hobbies, passions, and extracurricular activities. Are you a volunteer at an animal shelter? Do you play a sport or an instrument? Scholarships often exist for specific interests.

- Don't overlook niche scholarships. For example, if you're passionate about environmental science, search for scholarships offered by organizations dedicated to that cause. Smaller awards can also add up, so it's wise to apply for as many as you qualify for.

- Check out community organizations, local businesses, your school's financial aid office and even your parents' employers or unions. They frequently offer scholarships tailored to specific profiles, which might mean less competition for you compared to national contests.

Next, crafting compelling scholarship essays is crucial. A great essay tells your story in a way that stands out from the crowd. It's a chance to showcase your personal experiences, aspirations, and contributions in a way that makes the selection committee remember you. So what makes a scholarship essay stand out?

- Reflect on your life experiences and identify key moments that define you. Maybe volunteering has shaped your career goals, or an obstacle you've overcome shows your resilience.

- Always stick to the prompt. If the essay question is about leadership, focus on moments where you've led, whether it's in student government, a group project, or organizing a community event.

- Revise, revise, revise! Let your essay sit for a day or two, then come back to it with fresh eyes. Ask for feedback from teachers, family members, or friends. And remember, authenticity is key—let your true personality shine through.

Another vital component of a strong scholarship application is securing robust letters of recommendation. These letters can significantly bolster your application by providing evidence of your strengths from someone who knows you well. Here are some important tips on getting solid letters of recommendations:

- Choose recommenders who know you well and can speak positively about your abilities and character. Ideally, these should be teachers, mentors, or employers—not family members. Consider those who have seen you persevere through challenges, as they can write the most compelling letters.

- Request these letters well before the deadline. Give your recommenders at least two weeks' notice and make sure to provide them with all the necessary information about the scholarship and your accomplishments.

- Follow up respectfully. It's important to ensure they've submitted their letters on time. Sometimes a gentle reminder can go a long way.

Lastly, staying organized and meeting application deadlines is essential to maximizing your chances of receiving scholarship funds. Here's how you can stay on top of your applications:

- Use a calendar or planner to mark all scholarship deadlines. Ensure all important dates are visible and set reminders for upcoming due dates.

- Gather all necessary materials early. Last-minute applications often look rushed and incomplete, diminishing your chances of success.

- Submit your applications ahead of time. Websites can get clogged up near deadlines, so aim to submit at least a day or two early, if not a week early, to avoid any last-minute issues.

By mastering these steps, you'll not only reduce the financial burden of college tuition but also gain invaluable skills in organization, self-reflection, and communication. Remember, the effort you invest now can open doors to countless opportunities in the future.

There's a real relief of all or even part of your college expenses being covered because you took the time to organize, research, and present yourself in the best light possible. Scholarships can make a tangible difference in easing the financial pressures of higher education, allowing you to focus more on your studies and less on how you'll pay for them. So take the leap. Dive into the world of scholarships with confidence and determination.

Real-Life Success Stories of Scholarship Attainment

There are more than a few examples of those who've already won scholarships and are now thriving in college. These stories aren't just fluff; they're powerful narratives that can spark inspiration and action. Let's dive into some real-life success stories that might just motivate you to embark on your own scholarship journey.

We'll start with David. A native of Millersville, PA his ambitions led him beyond the borders of his hometown, landing him at Bloomsburg University. The financial support he received enabled him to fully immerse himself in his academic pursuits without the looming dread of debt.

Rosa, born in Phoenix, didn't have it easy growing up but always had big dreams. Her parents struggled, yet education was always a priority in her household. With the help of scholarships, Rosa earned her Bachelor's degree in Psychology despite facing initial difficulties in forming good study habits.

Another compelling example is Djdade, who grew up in the inner city and aspired to become an engineer. Scholarships provided him with the chance to explore environmental engineering and give back to his community. Through talks and coaching, he now inspires other kids from underprivileged backgrounds to pursue their dreams relentlessly.

Take Jenn, a Ph.D. student at Marquette University. Growing up as one of six children in inner-city conditions, college seemed like an unattainable dream until scholarships opened doors for her. She leveraged every opportunity—volunteering, networking, and excelling academically—to create a path where there seemingly was none.

What can you do to follow in their footsteps?

- Start by identifying scholarships that match your interests, background, and academic achievements.
- Prepare your applications meticulously. Highlight not just your academic qualifications but also extracurricular activities and personal stories that demonstrate resilience and determination.
- Seek feedback on your essays and applications. Often, a fresh perspective can catch errors or suggest improvements that can make your application shine.
- Apply to multiple scholarships. Don't put all your eggs in one basket. Cast a wide net to increase your chances of success.

These narratives are more than inspirational—they're practical roadmaps. They show that persistence, leveraging available resources, and sharing your unique experiences can pave the way to securing invaluable financial aid. So next time you're feeling uncertain about your college prospects, remember these stories. Let them fuel your determination and guide you towards your own scholarship success.

Begin to envision your own path. Understand that you can transform your dreams into reality with the right support. The journey might be challenging, but the rewards will be worth it—and your story could very well inspire the next group of students venturing down this path.

Summary

Achieving Financial Preparedness for College Success

As we wrap up this chapter about college funding, remember that understanding how to navigate the landscape of financial aid can make a world of difference in your academic journey. We've explored the essentials—the distinctions between grants, loans, and scholarships—and emphasized why it's crucial to start your research early. Armed with this knowledge, you're now better prepared to seek out and secure the funds necessary to support your higher education.

Remember there is a vast array of resources available to assist you. It's not just about browsing online platforms like Fastweb or speaking with your guidance counselor; it's about leveraging every single opportunity around you. By systematically searching and applying for these opportunities, you position yourself ahead of the game.

While diving into loans might seem daunting, being mindful of their long-term implications is key. Federal loans often provide more favorable terms compared to private loans, and understanding this distinction helps you make smarter borrowing decisions. Remember, it's about finding a balance—utilizing "free money" first before turning to loans, ensuring you borrow only what's absolutely necessary to cover essential expenses.

An effective financial plan involves bringing together various funding sources like pieces of a puzzle. Grants, scholarships, federal loans, work-study programs, and personal savings each play a role in painting a complete picture of how you'll finance your education. This approach not only lightens the financial burden but also allows you to focus more on your studies and less on financial worries.

For those concerned about the broader impacts, consider this: the choices you make today regarding college funding don't just affect your immediate future. They shape your financial health for years to come after graduation. Graduating with minimal debt opens up greater career flexibility and reduces stress, allowing you to pursue your passions without the constant pressure of paying off significant loans.

Finally, keep in mind that, as with everything in life, plans may evolve. New opportunities will arise, and staying flexible and proactive will help you adjust as needed. The path to funding your college education involves thorough research, strategic planning, and a commitment to seeking out every available resource.

So take a moment to absorb all this information and think about how it applies to your situation. Your journey towards funding your college education starts now—dig deep, stay organized, and be persistent. Conversations today could spark ideas tomorrow. With determination and the right approach, you'll pave the way for a fulfilling college experience, free from the weight of financial worries. Remember, this isn't just about covering tuition, it's about investing in your future, empowering you to achieve your dreams with confidence and stability.

CHAPTER 8

MASTERING THE ART OF RESPONSIBLE PURCHASING

We all have that one person in our family that knows how to find bargains! What makes someone a smart shopper? In this chapter, we'll explore how to master the art of responsible purchasing. It starts with establishing and sticking to your budget and includes other topics we've discussed previously, such as setting up a savings plan and an emergency fund. We'll provide practical tips and relatable examples to help you make informed decisions that balance your immediate desires with your future needs. By the end, you'll be equipped to differentiate between needs and wants, manage your spending wisely, and build a solid financial foundation that prepares you for whatever comes your way. Get ready to take control of your finances and make decisions that will serve you well in the long run.

Differentiating Between Needs and Wants

Understanding the difference between needs and wants is crucial not only for budgeting but also for making smart purchasing decisions. Needs are the essentials—items necessary for survival and well-being like food, shelter, clothing, and healthcare. Wants, on the other hand, are extras that make life more enjoyable but aren't essential for survival. By recognizing this distinction, you can prioritize spending on what truly matters first.

So you're eyeing a pair of sleek sneakers. They're tempting, offering an instant boost to your style, but then you remember your old, yet still functional, shoes at home. Do you need these new kicks, or do you just want them? This is exactly the kind of mindful decision-making we're going to explore here.

Here's where learning to distinguish between needs and wants really pays off. When you master this, each buying decision becomes a conscious one. It's about asking yourself key questions before reaching for your wallet: "Is this something I need right now, or can it wait?" This process not only helps you manage your money better but also gives you greater insight into what's driving your purchases.

Allocating resources intelligently means putting your needs front and center. Let's say you've listed your monthly expenses and identified the essentials like rent, food, and transportation. Once these are accounted for, you can allocate funds for your wants. By covering your necessities first, any leftover money can be spent on extras without guilt.

Regularly reassessing and reevaluating your needs versus wants isn't just a one-time task; it's an ongoing practice. As life changes, so do your priorities. What you considered a need last year might be downgraded to a want as circumstances evolve. Here's how you can keep your spending aligned with your long-term financial goals:

- Start by listing all your current expenses. Be honest with yourself about what falls under needs and what are simply nice-to-haves.

- Reevaluate your list regularly. Perhaps what seemed indispensable a few months ago isn't quite as critical now.

- Consider swapping high-cost items for their less expensive equivalents.

- Always assess whether the need will remain relevant in the future.

It's vital to understand this because life has its fair share of surprises—unexpected medical bills, car repairs, job loss. Having an emergency fund acts as a safety net, keeping you afloat during tough times. Think of it as your financial cushion, absorbing the shock when life's curveballs come your way. Establishing this fund begins with making room in your budget for regular contributions, ensuring it's there when you genuinely need it.

In practice, considering all this requires a bit of discipline. Before hitting 'buy' on that online cart, give yourself a moment to think. Is it adding value to your life, or is it an impulse-driven want? Sometimes a simple pause can help you differentiate between a fleeting desire and a genuine need.

Next time you're faced with a choice between grabbing fast food or cooking at home, remember it's not just about the meal—it's about recognizing the bigger picture of your financial health. Balancing immediate gratification with long-term stability is about making informed, conscious choices every step of the way.

Developing Smart Shopping Habits

Developing the habit of researching and comparing prices before making a purchase takes time, but it's worth the effort. It's easy to click 'buy' on the first online shop you land on, but take a moment, think about it and do some research. Thanks to endless options available online and in-store, you owe it to yourself to do a bit of homework first.

Browse multiple retailers for the same item. You'll be surprised how many times you'll save a couple of bucks simply by taking the time to do some research. There are several price-comparison tools like Google Shopping, Capital One Shopping and Karma or other apps designed specifically for this purpose.

Using price-comparison tools and seeking out discounts not only saves money but also makes you a smarter shopper. Nowadays, there's an app for almost everything, including finding deals. Tools like Honey or RetailMeNot can help you save a few dollars on your purchases.

Here's what you can do to tap into this:

- Download a couple of reputable price-comparison apps and explore their features.
- Sign up for email alerts from your favorite brands or stores.
- Don't forget cashback websites like Rakuten (formerly Ebates). You can earn back a percentage of what you spend on everyday items, which can add up over time.

Developing the skill of effective bargaining or negotiation when making big-ticket purchases can seem intimidating but is entirely manageable with a little practice. Think about buying something substantial, like a car or even a house. The sticker price or listing price isn't always set in stone. You have more power than you think to negotiate for a better deal.

Let's look at a major purchase like a car. First and foremost, do your research. Go into the conversation armed with information. Know your budget and what price you want and can afford to pay. Be polite but firm. And never, ever, settle for the first offer.

Creating and sticking to a shopping list is one of the simplest yet most impactful habits you can develop. It's all too easy to fall into the trap of impulse buys, especially when everything in a store seems perfectly curated to tempt you. But a shopping list is like having a financial GPS guiding you towards what you need without veering off course.

Here's what you can do to make the most of your shopping list:

- Before heading out, take stock of what you already have and write down what you truly need to buy.
- Write down only the essentials and approximate costs next to each item.
- Refer to the list while shopping, whether it's on your phone or paper.

By stopping impulse buys, you'll avoid those end-of-month scrambles where you wonder where all your money went. Lists anchor your financial plan and ensure every dollar spent aligns with your needs.

Adopting these cost-conscious shopping practices enhances your financial stewardship and maximizes the utility derived from each expenditure. When you consistently make informed purchasing decisions, use price-comparison tools, master the art of negotiation, and stick to planned lists, you're teaching yourself habits that can benefit you long-term. This approach isn't just about saving money, it's about cultivating a mindset that values thoughtful spending over spontaneous splurging.

Some stores offer student discounts. As a student, you may be entitled to several discounts and deals on everything from textbooks and school supplies to food and entertainment. Be sure to take advantage of these opportunities to save money. Many stores and businesses offer student discounts – just be sure to always have your student ID with you to take advantage of them.

Remember, it's not about being cheap; it's about being smart. Financial discipline today translates to more freedom and security tomorrow.

In today's economy, where everything seems overpriced and under-delivered, the ability to manage your finances wisely is invaluable. It puts the power back into your hands and gives you the confidence to navigate the consumer landscape with ease and efficiency. Apply these tips the next time you're about to make a purchase, no matter how small and you'll be surprised at the peace of mind it brings knowing you've made the best decision possible for your wallet and your future.

Creating a Personal Spending Plan

Creating a personal spending plan aligned with your financial goals may seem like an insurmountable task, especially when you're balancing school, a social life, and part-time work. But it's an incredibly enlightening and empowering exercise that can set you up for success in the future. Imagine having the freedom to buy what you want and still having savings stashed away for emergencies or future plans. It all starts with setting clear financial objectives.

Setting Clear Financial Objectives

What are you aiming for? These goals can be anything—saving for college, buying your first car, or simply having enough money to enjoy weekend outings with friends. Once you have these goals in mind, outlining a budget becomes simpler. The budget acts as your roadmap, guiding you towards disciplined spending.

Budgets are important and can help you see the big picture when it comes to responsible purchasing. By setting clear financial objectives and creating a well-outlined budget, you'll find it easier to stick to disciplined spending. Think of your budget as a friendly guide who nudges you to make smart choices, rather than a strict enforcer.

Tracking and Reviewing Spending Patterns

Now that you've set your financial goals and outlined a budget, the next step is to track your expenses. Monitoring where your money goes can be quite revealing. You might discover those daily coffee runs are costing you more than you thought. Regularly reviewing your spending patterns allows you to adjust your budget according to changing priorities or income fluctuations.

You can keep on top of things by following simple steps:

- Use a budgeting app: Apps can make tracking expenses easier by categorizing your spending automatically.

- Keep receipts and bills: Collect all receipts and bills to see exactly where your money is going. You can then log these manually if apps are not your thing.

- Review monthly: At the end of each month, sit down and review your spending. Look at areas where you went overboard and identify categories where you saved.

This practice not only keeps you accountable but also makes you more aware of your habits, enabling you to make smarter financial decisions in the future.

Including Provisions for Savings and Emergency Funds

One crucial aspect of a robust spending plan is making provisions for savings and emergency funds. Including savings and investments in your plan fosters financial security and prepares you for future needs.

There's a simple approach to ensure you're covered:

- Start small, aim big: Begin by setting aside a small percentage of your income, say 10%, and gradually increase it as you get more comfortable.

- Automate savings: Set up automatic transfers to your savings account. When you don't see the money, you're less likely to spend it impulsively.

- Emergency fund first: Life is unpredictable. Prioritize building an emergency fund, ideally covering three to six months' worth of expenses. This fund should be easily accessible, like in a savings account.

- Explore investments: Once your emergency fund is sorted, consider low-risk investments. Even small contributions can grow substantially over time through compound interest.

When you build the habit of saving and investing early, you're effectively securing your financial future. Remember, it's not about how much you earn, but how much you save and invest wisely.

Periodically Revisiting and Revising the Spending Plan

Life changes, and so should your spending plan. Periodically revisiting and revising your budget ensures it remains reflective of your evolving financial aspirations and contingencies. Maybe you've picked up a new hobby, or your income has increased—your budget should accommodate these changes. Here's how to keep your budget in sync with your life:

- Set a revision schedule: Decide on a frequency for revisiting your budget—whether it's quarterly, bi-annually, or annually.

- Evaluate goals: Reassess your financial goals regularly. Have any new ones emerged? Are old ones still relevant?

- Adjust allocations: Based on your current financial situation, adjust allocations for different categories. Perhaps you need to allocate more to savings now than before.

- Track your spending: Start by listing out all your recurring expenses. Use a spreadsheet or a budgeting app to keep things organized.

- Categorize expenses: Break them down into needs and wants. Essentials like rent, utilities, and groceries fall into needs, while entertainment and dining out fall into wants.

- Evaluate each expense: Ask yourself if each subscription is providing value. If it's something you don't use regularly, consider canceling it. If you find yourself, splurging for that specialty coffee too many times in one week, consider cutting it down to once a week as a special treat.

- Set reminders: In addition to making it a habit to review your subscriptions every few months, make note of when they renew if they renew annually. Then, about a month before they renew, re-evaluate them. This way, you won't find yourself paying for something you no longer use.

- Compare alternatives: For essential services, shop around. Sometimes switching providers or bundling services can save you money.

- Stay informed: Keep yourself updated with financial literacy resources to make informed adjustments. Websites like Penn's Financial Wellness and Yale's Financial Literacy pages offer excellent advice.

A dynamic budget that evolves with your circumstances will serve you better than a rigid one that doesn't reflect your current needs.

Key Takeaways

By now, it should be clear that developing and sticking to a personalized spending plan doesn't just help you manage money—it helps you attain your goals and cultivates responsible financial habits. From setting clear financial objectives and tracking expenses to saving diligently and revising your plan periodically, each step builds your financial perception and helps you manage your money better.

In essence, your spending plan is your partner in navigating the sometimes difficult path of financial responsibility. It equips you with the skills needed to balance economic growth and human welfare, ensuring you're prepared for whatever life throws your way. Starting these habits now will give you a head start in achieving both personal freedom and social responsibility in your financial journey.

Managing and Reducing Unnecessary Expenses

One of the best ways to get a handle on your money is by conducting a thorough review of your recurring expenses. Once you've taken stock of your recurring expenses, implementing strategies to minimize daily costs becomes easier. Simple lifestyle changes can go a long way in stretching your dollar further. Batch cooking, for instance, can save you both time and money by reducing food waste and minimizing the number of times you dine out.

Similarly, carpooling with friends or colleagues not only cuts down on fuel costs but also contributes to a healthier environment.

You can try these approaches:

- Batch cook meals: Spend time each week preparing meals in bulk. This not only saves money but ensures you have healthy and more economical options readily available, making it less tempting to order takeout.

- Carpool or use public transportation: Team up with friends who live nearby to share rides. You could also look at public transport options that might be cheaper than driving yourself.

- Consolidate subscriptions: Share services like Spotify or Amazon Prime with family or roommates. This can drastically reduce your monthly bills.

- Review your monthly subscriptions often: This can be an eye-opening exercise, as you'll often find that many small charges add up over time. Whether it's that gym membership you haven't used in months or multiple streaming services you hardly watch, identifying these and cancelling them puts the extra money in your pocket.

Practicing mindful consumption habits, particularly when it comes to impulse purchases, can make a significant difference in your budget. The lure of instant gratification can often lead to unnecessary expenses. Developing the skill of delayed gratification can help curb these tendencies, ensuring that your spending aligns more closely with your real needs and long-term goals.

Here's how to practice mindful spending:

- Sleep on it: If you're tempted to buy something on a whim, wait 24 hours before making the purchase. Often, the urge will pass, and you'll save money.

- Set budget limits: Decide in advance how much you're willing to spend on non-essential items each month. Stick to this limit to avoid overspending.

- Prioritize needs over wants: When shopping, ask yourself if the item is a need or a want. Always focus on buying what you truly need first.

- Cash-only rule: For impulse buys, stick to using cash. Swiping a credit card is easy. It's harder to part with physical money, which can deter frivolous purchases.

Exploring DIY (Do It Yourself) alternatives can also be incredibly rewarding for some people. Not only do you save money, but you also gain new skills and a sense of accomplishment. Learn to do basic car maintenance, like changing your oil, air filter, or windshield wipers. Make handmade gifts for birthdays or holidays, such as baked goods, candles, or personalized photo albums, rather than spending on store-bought items. Start a small indoor or outdoor herb garden to grow your own herbs and vegetables, reducing grocery costs.

Thrift shopping can also be a treasure trove for finding quality items at a fraction of their original cost. Swapping goods with friends or participating in community swap events can further extend your savings while fostering a sense of community.

Take a look around at the things you own but no longer need. Instead of throwing them out, you can sell those items online and make some money to turn around and buy things you now need. Clothes, electronics, books, and furniture are just a few things that can be resold easily on platforms like eBay, Facebook Marketplace, or apps like Poshmark. Not only will you clear up space in your home, but you'll also give your old belongings a second life while putting money back in your pocket. Use those same platforms and consider buying second-hand items from them. You can often find goods that you need (or want) at a fraction of the retail price. Buying and selling second hand is a also great way to practice sustainability by reducing waste.

Some tips to embrace DIY and thrifting:

- DIY projects: Look up tutorials online for simple projects like making your own cleaning products or repairing minor home issues.
- Thrifting: Visit local thrift stores or online marketplaces to find gently used items at a lower price. This is great for clothing, electronics, furniture, and even books.
- Swapping: Organize or participate in swap meets where you can exchange items you no longer need for things you want. This is especially useful for clothing and accessories.
- Use online platforms: Monetize the stuff you no longer need or want to buy things you now need or want.

Lastly, let's talk about emergency funds. Having an emergency fund is crucial for financial security. Life is unpredictable, and having a safety net can prevent unforeseen expenses from derailing your financial plan. Whether it's a medical emergency, car repair, or sudden job loss, an emergency fund ensures that you're prepared for unexpected situations without resorting to using a high-interest credit cards or applying for loans.

To build an emergency fund:

- Start small: Set aside a small amount each week. Even $5 or $10 can add up over time.
- Automate savings: Set up an automatic transfer from your checking account to a savings account dedicated to emergencies. This way, you'll save consistently without having to think about it.
- Cut unnecessary expenses: Use the savings from cutting daily costs to grow your emergency fund faster.
- Set a goal: Ideally, aim to save three to six months' worth of living expenses. This provides a comfortable buffer for most unexpected events.

Managing and reducing unnecessary expenses involves a combination of reviewing recurring costs, adopting cost-saving strategies, practicing mindful consumption, exploring DIY and thrifting, and building an emergency fund. By integrating these practices, you not only improve your financial health but also develop responsible habits that will serve you well throughout life. Every small step counts, and before you know it, you'll be more financially secure and empowered to make informed decisions.

Summary

Ensuring Financial Stability and Preparedness

As we wrap up our journey through making informed and responsible purchase decisions, it's essential to remember how crucial differentiating between needs and wants really is. By now, you should feel more confident about figuring out whether those new sneakers are a necessity or just a nice-to-have. Prioritizing your needs first ensures you're building a strong financial foundation, which is the key to long-term security and happiness.

We also dove into how creating and sticking to a personal spending plan can be a game changer. How you should have clear goals and a budget guiding you towards them. This isn't just about being restrictive; it's about being smart with your money. Tracking your expenses, allocating funds for savings, and periodically revisiting your budget helps keep your finances aligned with your evolving life.

Developing a budget helps to develop smart shopping habits that make every dollar count. From comparing prices and seeking deals to mastering negotiation skills, these practices ensure you're always getting the best value. It's like being equipped with a secret toolkit— one that transforms you into a savvy shopper, capable of navigating even the trickiest consumer landscape.

And then there's the importance of an emergency fund. It might not seem urgent now, but life has a way of throwing curveballs when you least expect it. Setting aside a small amount regularly will build a safety net, offering you peace of mind and financial stability during unexpected times.

It's all about balance. Yes, it's okay to enjoy life's little luxuries occasionally, but always make sure your essentials are covered first. By continuously asking yourself, "Do I need this right now, or can it wait?" you're training yourself to make thoughtful, conscious choices that benefit your overall financial health.

So next time you're weighing a purchase or planning your budget, remember these strategies. Life may be unpredictable, but taking control of your financial decisions provides a sense of preparedness and resilience.

As you move forward, think of these concepts as tools, ready to be used whenever needed. With the right approach to managing your money, you'll be ready for whatever comes your way. Make informed choices, save wisely, and embrace the journey of responsible financial management. The power is truly in your hands.

CHAPTER 9

UNDERSTANDING INSURANCE AND IDENTITY PROTECTION

Imagine waking up as a kid to find someone had broken your piggy bank into smithereens and taken all the money you had inside. You would be upset, right? Now, picture that same scenario as an adult, but instead of a piggy bank, it's your bank account. Someone uses your money or credit card to buy expensive items, steals your identity, and leaves you with debt that isn't yours. Growing up brings more responsibilities, and learning how to protect yourself from life's unexpected twists is part of that journey.

One major aspect of this responsibility involves knowing about insurance and why it's so important. Think of insurance as a safety net for when things go wrong. If you get sick and need to see a doctor, health insurance prevents medical bills from wiping out your savings. Without auto insurance, even a small car accident could drain your wallet. And don't count on your landlord's insurance to cover your belongings if you're renting; their insurance covers their asset—their building. You'll need renters insurance to cover damage to your assets—your possessions. Another critical issue young adults face today is identity theft—a sneaky crime where someone steals your personal information to commit fraud. The consequences are real and can include drained bank accounts or ruined credit scores, in some extreme cases arrest warrants, which can take years to sort out.

In this chapter, we'll cover the basics of different types of insurance—health, auto, and renters—and talk about why each one matters. We'll also explore practical steps you can take to guard against identity theft. By the end of this chapter, you'll have clear strategies and useful tips to help you make smart decisions now and throughout your life, ensuring you're not caught off guard by financial surprises or digital threats.

The Importance of Various Types of Insurance

Understanding different types of insurance might seem challenging, but breaking them down makes it simpler. Let's take a look at health, auto, and renters insurance.

Health insurance is like having extra lives in a video game. When you fall ill or get injured, health insurance covers medical bills that would otherwise be overwhelming to patch you right up. A single hospital visit without insurance could wipe out months of savings and leave you in debt.

Auto insurance is like armor for your car. Whether you're new behind the wheel or an experienced driver, accidents happen. Even a minor fender bender can lead to hefty repair costs. Auto insurance ensures that those expenses don't come straight out of your pocket. It covers not just repairs, but sometimes medical expenses if you're hurt in an accident. And if your car is stolen, insurance will compensate you so that you can buy another one.

The most basic type of coverage is liability-only insurance, which helps cover costs if you're at fault in an accident and need to pay for the other person's injuries or property damage. Liability-only coverage is the basic level of insurance required by law in most states. However, it doesn't cover any damage to your own car. Other options include comprehensive and collision coverage, which help pay for damage to your car, whether it's from an accident, theft, or things like hail or hitting a tree. These extra coverages give more protection but also cost more than liability-only

Having comprehensive coverage and collision coverage can get costly. However, the protection it offers can be especially important for young drivers who may not have the savings to cover unexpected collision repair costs out of pocket. Understanding these differences can help you make an informed decision about what type of coverage is right for you. Your decision should come down to what you can afford and does it provide you with the protection you need.

Renters insurance is essential if you're renting your home. Your landlord's insurance covers the building but not your personal belongings. Renters insurance steps in where your landlord's policy doesn't—it covers personal property inside your rented space and provides liability protection in case someone gets injured while visiting you.

Why do we need insurance? Simply put, insurance serves as a financial safety net during unexpected events. When unpleasant surprises pop up—like accidents, illnesses, or theft—insurance helps you manage the financial fallout and bounce back more smoothly. It gives peace of mind knowing that you won't face a financial crisis due to unforeseen circumstances.

Choosing the right insurance can feel overwhelming because there are so many options. Here's what you can do:

- Assess your risks: Are you driving often? Consider comprehensive auto insurance. Do you live in a busy neighborhood where theft is common? Renters insurance might be essential for you.
- Evaluate your budget: How much can you comfortably afford to spend on premiums each month? While a high deductible may mean a lower premium now, it will mean higher out-of-pocket expenses later if you have a claim.
- Research different policies: Not all insurance plans are created equal. Shop around, get multiple quotes, and compare them carefully.
- Read the fine print: Understand what is covered and what is not. Insurance policies often have exclusions that limit coverage.

Understanding these basics empowers you to make informed decisions when you reach adulthood, ensuring you know exactly what to look for and how to protect yourself financially.

Understanding Life and Disability Insurance

Life and disability insurance might not be on your radar yet, but understanding them now can prepare you for the future. These insurances provide financial protection against unforeseen events that could significantly impact your and your family's financial stability.

Life Insurance

Life insurance provides financial support to your loved ones in the event of your death. It's not something most young adults think about, but it can be crucial if you have dependents who rely on your income. You pay a regular premium, and if you pass away during the policy term, your beneficiaries receive a lump-sum payment. This money can help cover funeral costs, pay off debts, or provide for your family's living expenses.

There are several types of life insurance but let's look at just two types: term life and whole life.

Term Life Insurance: It provides coverage for a specific period, such as 10, 20, or 30 years. It's generally more affordable and straightforward. If you outlive the policy, there's no payout. Term life can be ideal for a young couple with a growing family. If something happens to one partner, the funds from a term life policy can help pay off the mortgage, providing the surviving spouse financial relief during a difficult time.

It can also be used as collateral for a loan. Using term life insurance as collateral for a loan is a way to secure the loan and give lenders confidence that they'll be repaid, even if something happens to you. In this case, the lender becomes the beneficiary of the policy for the amount of the loan. If you pass away during the loan term, the insurance payout will first go towards paying off the remaining loan balance, and any leftover amount would go to your designated beneficiaries. It's a common practice when applying for larger loans, such as a business loan, to ensure the lender gets repaid in the event of your death.

Whole Life Insurance: It covers you for your entire life and includes an investment component, which can build cash value over time. It's more expensive but offers lifelong coverage and potential financial growth. This type of insurance is best for someone who wants to provide lifelong protection for their family.

While you might not need life insurance right now, it's something to consider once you have financial dependents or significant debts that could burden your family.

Disability Insurance

Disability insurance replaces your income if you can't work due to illness or injury. Imagine you get into an accident and can't work for several months. Without a regular paycheck, how would you cover your living expenses? Disability insurance steps in to fill this gap.

There are two main types of disability insurance: short-term and long-term.

Short-Term Disability Insurance: It covers a portion of your income for a few months, typically three to six months, following a disabling event.

Long-Term Disability Insurance: It kicks in after short-term coverage ends and can provide benefits for several years, up to retirement age, depending on the policy.

Employers often offer disability insurance as part of their benefits package, but you can also purchase individual policies. Having disability insurance ensures that you can maintain your financial stability and continue meeting your obligations even if you're temporarily unable to work.

Why Learn About These Insurances Now?

Even though you might not need life and disability insurance immediately, knowing about them early on helps you make informed decisions when the time comes. As you progress in your career and start a family, these types of insurance become more relevant. Understanding their benefits and how they work will allow you to protect yourself and your loved ones effectively, ensuring long-term financial security. This proactive approach can save you time, money, and stress, providing peace of mind that you're covered no matter what life throws your way.

Finding Affordable Insurance Coverage

Finding affordable insurance without sacrificing coverage involves smart research and understanding your options. Whether you're dealing with health insurance or car insurance, knowing where to look and what questions to ask can make all the difference.

First, research and compare insurance policies from different providers. This might sound tedious, but a little effort here goes a long way. Check multiple sources and use online comparison tools to simplify the process. Read customer reviews and consult financial advisors for valuable insights.

Understanding the factors that influence insurance premiums is crucial. Premiums can vary widely based on age, health status, location, type of coverage, and lifestyle choices. Even your credit score can impact the premium you'll pay on insurance. Knowing these factors helps you take steps to lower your costs.

Exploring discounts and bundling options can save you even more. Many insurers offer discounts for good students, safe drivers, and multi-policy holders. Always ask your insurance provider if there are any discounts you might be eligible for.

Finally, reading and understanding insurance policies ensures you get adequate coverage. Look for exclusions and limitations, clarify terms, and keep an eye on the renewal dates. Evaluating your policies annually ensures they still meet your needs.

By following these strategies, you can find insurance policies that are both affordable and comprehensive enough to keep them protected. Balancing cost and coverage doesn't have to be overwhelming once you get the hang of it.

Protecting Against Identity Theft

Equally important to securing insurance is protecting yourself against identity theft. In today's digital age, personal information can easily be compromised if you don't take proper precautions. Identity theft happens when someone steals your personal data—like your Social Security Number or credit card info—and uses it fraudulently. The consequences can be severe, ranging from drained bank accounts to ruined credit scores.

To safeguard against identity theft, consider adopting these practices:

- Be cautious with your personal information: Don't share your Social Security Number unless absolutely necessary, and shred documents containing sensitive details before discarding them.

- Strengthen your online security: Use strong, unique passwords mixing letters, numbers and special characters for different accounts and enable two-factor authentication where possible. Two-factor authentication is when a website sends you a code either your cell phone or your email that you have to enter along with your password to access your account. The most commonly used passwords are "Password", "Password123" and "Pa55word" – if either of those are any of your passwords, stop reading this book, go change it right now and come back!

- Monitor your financial statements and credit reports: Regularly checking these can help catch any suspicious activity early. Many banks and credit reporting agencies send alerts for unusual transactions, allowing you to act swiftly before significant damage is done. Sign up for them if available!

- Report suspicious activity immediately: If you suspect your information has been compromised, report it to relevant authorities and your financial institutions. They can guide you through the steps to secure your accounts and minimize potential harm.

Understanding how identity thieves steal personal information is also essential. They use techniques like phishing, dumpster diving, skimming, and hacking into weak passwords. Being aware of these methods helps you stay vigilant and take proactive steps to protect your data.

Avoiding Financial Scams

Learning to identify and avoid financial scams is crucial for young adults. Scammers often target teens with fake job offers, bogus scholarships, or "too good to be true" online sales. Red flags include unsolicited messages promising big rewards with minimal effort and requests for personal information upfront.

To protect yourself, be skeptical of offers that sound too good to be true. Always double-check who you're dealing with, verify URLs and email addresses, and research the company or person making the offer. Always read the fine print and consult trusted adults or official resources if you're unsure.

Let's look at some common scams targeting teens and young adults. Fake scholarship offers are a big one. Scammers prey on your desire to afford college, offering huge sums of money for minimal effort. Usually, these require processing fees or personal info, and once you pay or provide what they ask, poof—they disappear.

Another prevalent scam involves flashy online stores selling knock-off designer goods. You think you're getting a deal, but either the product never arrives, or you receive a cheap imitation. Employment scams are also rampant. These might request upfront fees for training materials or charge for background checks—no real employer would do this. Reports reveal these scams have surged since the pandemic, indicating the necessity for vigilance.

Unfortunately, even following these tips doesn't guarantee full protection. The truth of the matter is either you or someone close to you will be a victim of some type of identity theft at some point in your life. What should you do? Take action immediately! Your proactiveness can help minimize the damage.

Here's a step-by-step guide on what to do:

- Contact your bank and credit card companies: Inform them about the fraud. They'll freeze your accounts and help you navigate next steps.

- File a report with the Federal Trade Commission (FTC): The FTC will help you create a recovery plan.

- Place fraud alerts on your credit reports: Contact one of the three major credit bureaus (Experian, TransUnion, or Equifax) to place a fraud alert. This makes it harder for thieves to open new accounts in your name.

- Create an identity theft report: Visit IdentityTheft.gov to put together a recovery plan based on your specific situation.

- Notify the police: File a police report with your local department. This usually helps with legal and official issues related to clearing your name.

By understanding the risks of identity theft and implementing proactive measures, you can seriously lower your chances of becoming a victim and protect yourself from financial fraud and privacy breaches.

Eva, a young college student, was aware of the growing threat of identity theft, especially for young adults managing new financial responsibilities like student loans and part-time jobs. She decided to take proactive steps to protect her personal information after hearing about a friend whose identity had been stolen. She set up strong, unique passwords for all her online accounts. She signed up for credit monitoring alerts through her bank, so she would be notified of any unusual activity right away. In addition, she made a habit of shredding any sensitive documents before throwing them away, including bank statements, bills, and anything with her Social Security Number.

By taking these simple but effective measures, Eva significantly reduced her risk of falling victim to identity theft. Her proactive steps gave her peace of mind, knowing she had done everything possible to protect her personal and financial information. Being proactive, even with small changes, can greatly lower the risk of identity theft and safeguard one's financial future.

If you're still not convinced that safeguarding your identity is worth the time and effort, consider this: More than 950,000 Americans lost nearly $2 billion to identity thieves last year alone. The average loss was almost $1,000, but there are cases where people lost over $10,000. Imagine the stress of trying to recover from that, especially if you're just starting out in life.

Summary

Protecting Yourself and Your Identity

Understanding insurance and identity protection can save you a lot of headaches down the road. Different types of insurance—health, auto, and renters—act as defense mechanisms in a game with both predictable and surprise challenges. Choosing the right insurance based on your needs and risks ensures you're not just throwing money at policies but making smart choices.

Protecting your identity involves being vigilant online and offline. Limit what you share, strengthen security measures, and monitor your financial accounts regularly to help keep your personal information safe.

By grasping the importance of various types of insurance and taking proactive measures to protect against identity theft, you're in a position to navigate life's uncertainties with greater confidence. Ensuring your financial safety net is in place is a significant step towards responsible adulthood, paving the way for a more secure future. It's about turning knowledge into action, making informed choices, and building good habits that serve you well both now and later.

Chapter 10

Traveling Affordably Without Sacrificing Quality

Time to delve into one of the fun things you can do with your money....travel! Traveling affordably without sacrificing quality is a balancing act that many young adults strive to master. It's about seeking out the best deals, making informed choices, and being flexible enough to adapt to opportunities as they arise. The allure of exploring new places doesn't have to come with a hefty price tag if you know how to navigate the world of budget travel efficiently.

So whether it's planning the ultimate senior year trip, wanting to see a different part of the country or world or just getting back home during a school break, in this chapter, you'll discover practical tips and strategies to secure cheap flights and transportation options. You'll learn how to effectively use flight comparison websites, take advantage of budget airlines, and book your travel well in advance to snag the best deals. Additionally, the chapter will cover how to utilize airline rewards programs to further stretch your travel budget. With these insights, young adventurers can embark on memorable journeys without compromising on comfort or breaking the bank.

Finding and Booking Cheap Flights and Transportation Options

Traveling doesn't have to break the bank, especially when you know how to find great deals on flights and transportation. By leveraging smart strategies, you can enjoy their adventures without sacrificing comfort or quality.

In today's digital age, flight comparison websites are a traveler's best friend. Websites like Skyscanner, Google Flights, and Kayak enable users to compare prices from multiple airlines on a single platform. This makes it easier to spot significant price differences, ensuring you snag the best deal available. For instance, by entering your travel dates into one of these sites, you can view a list of options from various airlines, allowing you to compare prices, flight durations, and layover times all at once.

It's also important to take advantage of the alert features many comparison sites offer. Setting up price alerts for specific routes or destinations can give you a heads-up when ticket prices drop, helping you book at the optimal time. This feature is particularly useful if you have flexible travel plans, as it allows you to adapt and choose the most cost-effective dates. Taking a few moments to set these alerts can result in substantial savings.

Another tip is to use incognito mode or clear your browser cookies when revisiting these comparison sites. Sometimes, repeated searches for the same route can lead to price hikes due to dynamic pricing algorithms. Staying incognito ensures that the prices you see remain unbiased and purely reflective of market changes rather than your search habits.

Opting for Budget Airlines

Budget airlines present another fantastic way to save money on air travel. Carriers such as Spirit, Southwest, Ryanair, and EasyJet offer no-frills services at significantly reduced fares compared to mainstream airlines. While these airlines may not provide the same level of luxury, they ensure you reach your destination at a fraction of the cost. It's essential to research which budget airlines operate in your region and consider them as viable options.

When flying with budget airlines, be mindful of additional fees. Many low-cost carriers charge extra for checked baggage, seat selection, and even onboard snacks. To maximize your savings, pack light and stick to carry-on luggage whenever possible. Bring your own snacks and entertainment to avoid paying extra onboard. Understanding and navigating these potential add-ons can transform a seemingly cheap ticket into genuine savings.

Booking in Advance

One of the most effective ways to secure affordable flights is to book well in advance. Airlines tend to release their flight schedules and ticket sales about a year ahead, and the initial prices are often the lowest you'll find. Booking at least three, if not six months before your trip typically provides the best rates. By planning your travel early, you allow yourself ample time to watch for fluctuations and act when the prices are favorable.

Planning ahead also offers the benefit of a broader selection. You're more likely to find seats on your preferred flights, ensuring better departure times and fewer layovers. Early bookings also give you the flexibility to adjust dates slightly to capitalize on cheaper fares. This proactive approach removes the stress of last-minute searches, where limited options can drive prices up significantly.

However, if your travel plans aren't solidified months in advance, don't panic. Some airlines also offer some great last-minute deals if you're willing to be flexible on your dates and your destination. Always keep an eye on policies regarding cancellations or changes to ensure any adjustments don't incur heavy fees.

Utilizing Rewards Programs

Harnessing airline rewards programs can significantly lower travel expenses. Many airlines offer loyalty programs that reward frequent flyers with points or miles that can be redeemed for free flights, upgrades, and other perks. Signing up for these programs typically costs nothing and yields long-term benefits for avid travelers. Accumulating points can quickly translate into substantial savings, enhancing the overall value of your trips.

Maximize these programs by consolidating your flights with one or two airlines. Building loyalty with a particular carrier from a young age lets you accumulate rewards faster, leading to premium benefits like priority boarding, free checked bags, and access to exclusive lounges. If you're a student or young adult frequently traveling, researching which airlines offer the best rewards programs tailored to your needs is worth the extra effort.

Additionally, many credit cards partner with airlines to offer travel rewards. For example, some American Express cards offer Delta Air Lines reward miles, some Barclays cards offer JetBlue reward miles. Using a co-branded airline credit card for your everyday purchases can boost your points accumulation significantly. These cards often come with bonus points for signing up, further discounts on airfares, and perks like free checked bags or travel insurance. Smart usage of these financial tools can amplify your travel budget, making distant destinations more accessible.

By incorporating these simple strategies while planning your travel, securing affordable flights and transportation becomes a manageable task. Utilize flight comparison websites, consider budget airlines, book in advance, and make the most of rewards programs to explore the world without compromising quality. Your next adventure awaits, and with these tips, it can be both memorable and budget-friendly.

Selecting Budget-Friendly Accommodations Without Compromising Comfort and Safety

Exploring alternative accommodations is an essential strategy for traveling affordably without compromising on comfort. Hostels have become a popular choice, especially among young adults and backpackers. They offer a social atmosphere where you can meet fellow travelers from around the world while saving money. Hostels come in various forms; some provide private rooms, while others have dormitory-style setups. This flexibility allows you to choose what best fits your budget and privacy preferences. When considering them, think safety first - do your research, check reviews and see what others say about their stay there.

Homestays are another fantastic option. By staying with local families, you not only save on accommodation costs but also gain a unique cultural experience. Hosts often provide insider tips about the area, which can enrich your travel experience. Platforms like Airbnb offer a wide range of homestays, catering to different needs and budgets. Often, meals might be included, or hosts may guide you to authentic local eateries, further enhancing your stay and cultural experience.

Guesthouses provide a middle ground between hostels and hotels. They usually offer more privacy than hostels and can be more comfortable than some homestays. Guesthouses tend to be family-owned, giving them a cozy, home-like feel while still being affordable. Many guesthouses provide amenities similar to those found in hotels, such as Wi-Fi, breakfast, and laundry services, ensuring a comfortable stay without the hefty price tag of a hotel.

Using accommodation booking platforms can unlock significant savings. Websites and apps like Booking.com, Hostelworld, and Agoda specialize in finding discounted rates. These platforms often run promotions and provide user reviews to help you make informed decisions. Filters allow you to sort options by price, location, and amenities, ensuring you find lodging that meets your specific needs.

Another advantage of using these platforms is, again, their loyalty programs. Many offer points or discounts for frequent users, which can add up to substantial savings over time. Additionally, last-minute deals are often available, ideal for spontaneous travelers. Comparing prices across multiple platforms ensures you get the best possible rate, so always check several before making a final booking.

Many of these platforms also include cancellation policies and customer support, offering peace of mind if your plans change. Always read the fine print regarding cancellations and refunds, ensuring you won't lose money if adjustments are necessary. By leveraging these online tools, you can secure quality accommodation without straining your budget.

Reading reviews and ratings is crucial when selecting budget accommodation. Online feedback from previous guests provides valuable insights into the safety, cleanliness, and overall quality of a place. High ratings and positive comments are strong indicators of a reliable and comfortable stay. On the other hand, consistently poor reviews should serve as red flags.

Take time to read both recent and older reviews to get a comprehensive picture. Recent reviews reflect the current state of the accommodation, while older ones can show long-term trends. Pay attention to common themes in feedback, such as issues with cleanliness or noise levels, as these are likely accurate reflections of the property's conditions.

Photos posted by previous guests can also be informative. Official photos on listing sites may not always accurately represent the property. User-uploaded images give a more realistic view, helping you set proper expectations. Combining reviews and photos will enable you to make a well-informed decision that balances affordability with comfort.

Planning Cost-Effective Itineraries to Maximize Experiences on a Limited Budget

When planning a budget-friendly trip, it's crucial to start by prioritizing activities. This means identifying the must-see attractions and allocating your budget in a way that ensures you don't miss out on these highlights. Make a list of the top experiences you want to have and rank them by importance. This will help you focus your spending on what truly matters to you.

Once you've identified your must-see attractions, consider how much each activity will cost and allocate your budget accordingly. For example, if visiting a famous museum is a priority, factor in the entrance fee and perhaps even set aside some money for a meal or souvenir from the museum's gift shop. By budgeting for these key activities in advance, you ensure that you won't be caught off guard by unexpected expenses.

It's also helpful to look for discounts or bundled deals for these attractions. Many tourist destinations offer city passes, hop on hop off buses or attraction packages that can save you money while allowing you access to multiple sites. Do some research online or ask locals for recommendations on the best deals. This strategic approach will help you make the most of your budget without compromising on quality experiences.

In addition to prioritizing paid attractions, research free or low-cost activities available at your destination. Most cities have numerous hidden gems that don't require an entry fee. Parks, beaches, public markets, and walking tours are often great ways to experience a new place without spending too much money. These activities not only help stretch your budget but often provide a more authentic feel of the local culture.

Start by doing some research on travel blogs and websites dedicated to budget travel. Look for articles about your destination that highlight free events or attractions. You might discover local festivals, free museum days, or community events that align with your travel dates. Such experiences can offer memorable moments without the hefty price tag.

Don't hesitate to reach out to locals for suggestions. Platforms like Couchsurfing and Meetup allow you to connect with residents who may share insider tips on inexpensive activities. You might find yourself invited to a local gathering or shown around town by someone passionate about their city. Finding these opportunities enhances your travel experience while keeping costs down.

Here's where you can take your budgeting skills to the next level. Creating a daily budget is another essential step in traveling affordably without sacrificing quality. Start by estimating your total travel expenses, including accommodation, transportation, food, and entertainment. Once you have a general idea of your overall trip cost, break it down into a daily allowance. This practice helps you maintain control over your spending throughout your journey.

Use budgeting apps to keep track of your expenses. Tools such as Trail Wallet or Budget Your Trip can help monitor your daily spending, making adjustments easier as needed. Set realistic limits for your daily expenditures, accounting for both expected costs and a small buffer for unexpected expenses. Sticking to this plan ensures you don't run out of funds before your trip ends.

Planning your meals can be part of your daily budget strategy. Opt for affordable dining options like street food stands, local markets, or cooking some meals yourself if you have access to kitchen facilities. Research ahead to find budget-friendly restaurants known for offering good value for money. Allocating a specific portion of your daily budget for food helps prevent overspending. And if there's a trendy, high end place that you must go to – skip lunch and save your appetite and money for a nice dinner!

Utilizing public transportation is a highly effective way to save money while getting around your destination. Instead of relying on taxis or ride-sharing services, explore the local public transit options such as buses, trains, or trams. These modes of transport are generally much cheaper and can give you a more immersive experience of the local way of life.

Invest in a travel card or pass if your destination offers one. Many cities provide tourists with unlimited access to their public transportation system for a set number of days at a discounted rate. This can be a cost-effective solution, especially if you plan to move around frequently. Familiarize yourself with the local transit schedules, fares and routes to maximize efficiency.

Walking or biking can be another great alternative for short distances. Not only does it save money, but it also allows you to explore the area at a leisurely pace, discovering places you might otherwise miss. Many cities have bike-sharing programs that are both economical and convenient. Take advantage of these options to reduce your transportation costs while enjoying the scenery.

Summary

Traveling Near and Far Within Your Budget

In this chapter, we've explored various ways to travel affordably without giving up comfort or quality. With the right strategies, young adults can embark on exciting journeys and create lasting memories without draining their bank accounts. By now, you should have a good grasp of how to find cheap flights and transportation options, from utilizing flight comparison websites and budget airlines to booking in advance and leveraging rewards programs.

Remember the excitement of planning your trip! With all these practical tips at your fingertips, you can turn that excitement into an efficient plan. Whether you're setting up price alerts for flights, staying with local families through homestays, or using loyalty programs to score free flights, these techniques can stretch your travel budget further than you might have thought possible.

However, there are a few things you should be mindful of as you plan your travels. Dynamic pricing can affect your airfare if you're not careful with your search habits, and budget airlines often have hidden fees that can stack up quickly if you're unprepared. Also, keep in mind that while booking early generally saves you money, being flexible with your plans might lead to last-minute deals that rival those early bird rates.

Where will your next adventure take you? With these insights, you're well-equipped to explore the world, meet new people, and discover new cultures, all while keeping your finances in check.

Happy travels, and may your journeys be filled with incredible experiences and stories worth sharing!

CHAPTER 11

UNDERSTANDING BASIC BUSINESS FINANCIAL STATEMENTS AND TERMS

Learning about basic business financial statements is essential for anyone interested in running a business, investing, or just looking to understand how companies operate. These financial statements provide a clear picture of a company's financial health and help in making informed decisions. The three key financial statements everyone should know are the Balance Sheet, Profit and Loss Statement (also known as the Income Statement), and Cash Flow Statement. Let's break down what each one is and why it's important.

The Balance Sheet provides a snapshot of a company's stability by detailing its assets, liabilities, and shareholders' equity at a specific point in time. This helps determine whether the company has a solid financial foundation. The Income Statement shows the company's profitability over a period; it takes revenue, subtracts expenses and tells you if there is a profit or a loss. It not only answers the question of whether the business is making money or incurring losses, but when you compare the income statement from one year to another or from one quarter to another, it can show you if a business is growing or contracting. Finally, the Statement of Cash Flow tracks the flow of cash in and out of the business, divided into operating, investing, and financing activities. This statement is vital for understanding whether the company has enough money to meet its short-term obligations and continue its operations, effectively answering the question of whether the business can survive. Together, these statements provide a comprehensive view of a company's financial performance and position.

Balance Sheet

The Balance Sheet is a snapshot of a company's financial position. It shows what the company owns (assets), what it owes (liabilities), and the owner's equity (what the owners would have left if the company sold all its assets and paid off all its debts). Think of it as a financial report card that lists everything the company owns and owes.

The structure of a balance sheet is:

Assets = Liabilities + Equity

But you can also look at it as Assets - Liabilities = Equity, answering the question - do you own enough to cover your debts?

This equation must always balance, hence the name "Balance Sheet."

Assets are what you own:

- cash (including what is in the bank)
- inventory (goods available for sale)
- accounts receivable (what people owe you and you expect to collect someday)
- fixed assets (land, machinery, equipment, and buildings)

Liabilities are what you owe:

- accounts payable
- income taxes payable
- mortgages and long-term debt

If you sold all of your assets and then paid your liabilities, equity is what's left over. Equity is, essentially, the portion of a company's assets that is owned by the shareholders or the owners after all liabilities (debts) have been paid.

Equity on a balance sheet is not the exact value of a business The true market value of a business can be higher or lower than the equity shown on the balance sheet. This is because factors like future earnings potential, market conditions, and intangible assets (like brand reputation or intellectual property) are not always fully captured in the balance sheet. So, while equity is a useful indicator, it doesn't reflect the full market value of a business.

Let's breakdown the key components of the Balance Sheet a little deeper:

Assets: These are resources owned by the company that have value. They can be classified into two categories:

- Current Assets: These are assets that can be converted into cash within a year. Examples include cash, accounts receivable (money owed to the company by customers), inventory (goods available for sale), and short-term investments.

- Non-Current Assets: These are long-term assets that will not be converted into cash within a year. Examples include property, equipment, and intangible assets like patents and trademarks.

Liabilities: These are the company's debts or obligations. Like assets, liabilities can be classified into two categories:

- Current (or Short Term) Liabilities: These are debts that need to be paid within a year. Examples include accounts payable (money the company owes to suppliers), short-term loans, and accrued expenses (expenses that have been incurred but not yet paid).
- Non-Current (or Long Term) Liabilities: These are debts that do not need to be paid within a year. Examples include loans, bonds payable, and deferred tax liabilities.

Equity: This represents the owner's share of the company. It includes:

- Common Stock: This represents the value of the shares issued by the company.
- Retained Earnings: These are profits that have been reinvested in the business rather than distributed to the owners.
- Additional Paid-In Capital: This is any additional amount of money the owners have invested in the company.

Example:

Imagine you own a small business, your Balance Sheet might look something like this:

Assets:

- Cash: $5,000
- Accounts Receivable: $2,000
- Inventory: $3,000
- Equipment: $10,000

Liabilities:

- Accounts Payable: $2,000
- Short-Term Loan: $1,000
- Long-Term Loan: $5,000

Equity:

- Common Stock: $7,000
- Retained Earnings: $5,000

So, your Balance Sheet equation would be:

Assets ($20,000) = Liabilities ($8,000) + Equity ($12,000)

Profit and Loss Statement (Income Statement)

The Profit and Loss Statement, also known as the Income Statement, shows the company's financial performance over a specific period (like a month, quarter, or year). It summarizes the income as well as the costs and expenses incurred during that period to determine the net profit or loss.

The income statement tells you: Are you profitable? How much money do you make? What costs do you need to control?

Income statement structure

The structure of an income statement is Revenue – Expenses = Profit (or Loss)

Revenue is what you earn from sales of:

- Physical merchandise
- Revenue earned from services you provide
- Miscellaneous revenue, such as interest from a savings account

Expenses can be broken into two main categories:

- Cost of goods sold: what it costs you to manufacture or buy what you sell
- Overhead expenses: the costs required to run the business that aren't directly tied to revenue such as rent, salaries of employees, telephone expenses.

There are two categories of overhead expenses: fixed costs and variable costs.

Fixed costs are expenses that a business has to pay regardless of how much it produces or sells, and they remain constant over time. For example, rent for office or commercial space, salaries of permanent employees, and insurance premiums are fixed costs because they don't change with the level of business activity. Whether a business produces a lot or very little, these costs stay the same. If your rent is $12,000 per year, it's $12,000 per year whether you sell 5 or 100 units of product per day. Furthermore, you can't control what your rent amount is each month – it is what it is!

Variable costs, on the other hand, fluctuate based on the business's production or sales volume. For example, the cost of raw materials, shipping expenses, and hourly wages are variable costs. If a company produces more products, it will spend more on these items, and if it produces less, these costs will decrease.

Variable costs move up or down based on a level of activity. If every unit of product we sell requires a $1.00 box, the total cost of the boxes varies. If we sell 5 units, the total cost is $5.00 (5 x $1,00); if we sell 100 units, it costs $100.00 (100 x $1.00). Electricity, gas, and water used in manufacturing can vary depending on production levels. Furthermore, many times you can control variable costs, like your advertising, and increase them or decrease them as funds and your situation or business plan allows.

Let's breakdown the key components of the Profit and Loss Statement:

1. **Revenue:** This is the income the company earns from its operations, like sales of goods or services.
2. **Cost of Goods Sold (COGS):** This is the direct cost of producing the goods sold by the company. It includes the cost of materials and labor used to create the product.
3. **Gross Profit:** This is calculated by subtracting the COGS from the revenue. It shows how much money the

company makes from its core activities before deducting operating expenses.

4. **Operating Expenses:** These are the costs required to run the business that are not directly tied to the production of goods or services. Examples include rent, utilities, salaries, marketing, and depreciation.

5. **Operating Profit (EBIT):** This is calculated by subtracting operating expenses from gross profit. EBIT stands for Earnings Before Interest and Taxes.

6. **Net Profit (Net Income):** This is the final profit after all expenses, including interest and taxes, have been deducted from the operating profit.

Example:

Let's say your small business had the following financial activity for the year:

Revenue: $50,000

Cost of Goods Sold (COGS): $20,000

Your **Gross Profit** would be:

Gross Profit = $50,000 Revenue - $20,000 COGS = $30,000

Next, you have to account for operating expenses:

Operating Expenses:

- Rent: $5,000
- Utilities: $1,000
- Salaries: $10,000

- Marketing: $2,000

Your **Operating Profit (EBIT)** would be:

Operating Profit = $30,000 Gross Profit - $18,000 Operating Expenses ($5,000 + $1,000 + $10,000 + $2,000) = $12,000

Finally, subtract interest on any loans and taxes to find your **Net Profit**:

- Interest: $500
- Taxes: $1,500

Net Profit = $12,000 Operating Profit - $2000 Interest and Taxes ($500 + $1,500) = $10,000

Cash Flow Statement

The Cash Flow Statement is basically a report showing how much cash that you receive or use over a specific period of time. It breaks down how much cash your business brings in from operations (selling a product or service) and investments (for example, interest earned in a savings account) and how much cash your business needs to pay and fund its operations.

The Cash Flow Statement is divided into three main sections: Operating Activities, Investing Activities, and Financing Activities.

Key Components of the Cash Flow Statement:

1. **Operating Activities:** This section shows cash generated or used by the company's core business operations. It includes receipts from sales and payments for expenses like wages and supplies.

2. **Investing Activities:** This section shows cash used for or generated from investments in the business, like buying or selling equipment or property.

3. **Financing Activities:** This section shows cash flows related to borrowing or repaying loans, issuing or buying back shares, and paying dividends to shareholders.

Example:

Let's say your small business had the following cash flow activities for the month:

Operating Activities:

- Cash Receipts from Sales: $10,000
- Cash Payments for Expenses: $6,000

Net Cash from Operating Activities = Cash Receipts - Cash Payments

So, your expected Net Cash from Operating Activities would be $10,000 - $6,000 or $4,000

Emmi's Baking Business

Remember Emmi's baking business from Chapter 2? To ensure her business is profitable and successful, Emmi needs to keep a close eye on her financial statements: the Balance Sheet, Profit and Loss Statement, and Cash Flow Statement.

Balance Sheet

The Balance Sheet will help Emmi understand her business's financial position at any given time. Here's what she should focus on:

- **Assets:** Emmi's assets include cash, baking supplies (flour, sugar, chocolate chips, etc.), baking equipment (oven, mixers, baking trays), and any money owed to her from customers (accounts receivable).

- **Liabilities:** These are the amounts Emmi owes, such as money borrowed to buy ingredients or equipment, and any unpaid bills.

- **Equity:** This represents Emmi's investment in the business and any retained earnings (profit that she hasn't taken out yet).

By tracking her Balance Sheet, Emmi can see if her business is growing over time, how much she owes compared to what she owns, and whether her equity is increasing, indicating a profitable business.

Profit and Loss Statement (Income Statement)

The Profit and Loss Statement will show Emmi her revenue, expenses, and profit over a period, such as a month or a year.

- **Revenue:** This is the total money Emmi makes from selling her baked goods.

- **Cost of Goods Sold (COGS):** This includes the cost of ingredients and packaging for the baked goods she sells.

- **Operating Expenses:** These are the costs to run her business, like utilities, marketing, and any wages if she hires help.

- **Net Profit:** This is the amount left after all expenses are subtracted from the revenue.

By reviewing her Profit and Loss Statement, Emmi can determine if her pricing is correct, if she needs to control costs better, and ultimately, if she's making a profit.

Cash Flow Statement

The Cash Flow Statement shows the flow of cash in and out of Emmi's business.

- **Operating Activities:** Cash from selling baked products and cash paid for ingredients and expenses.
- **Investing Activities:** Cash spent on new baking equipment or repairs.
- **Financing Activities:** Any loans taken or repaid.

Tracking her Cash Flow Statement ensures Emmi can see if she has enough cash to cover her day-to-day expenses and if she needs to plan for any future investments or expenses.

Why It's Important:

For Emmi, understanding these financial statements helps her make informed decisions, such as when to buy more supplies, how to price her sweet treats, and whether she can afford to invest in better equipment or more advertising. It also helps her plan for the future, ensuring her business remains profitable and sustainable.

Christopher's Lawn Mowing and Snow Removal Business

Remember Christopher's lawn mowing/snow removal business? To manage his seasonal business effectively, Christopher needs to keep track of his financial statements as well.

Balance Sheet

Christopher's Balance Sheet will help him monitor his business's financial health.

- **Assets:** Christopher's assets include cash, lawn mowers, snow blowers, shovels, and other equipment, as well as accounts receivable from customers.
- **Liabilities:** These include any loans taken to buy equipment, unpaid bills, and other debts.
- **Equity:** This represents Christopher's investment in the business and retained earnings.

By maintaining his Balance Sheet, Christopher can track his assets, ensure he's not over-leveraged with debt, and monitor his business's growth.

Profit and Loss Statement (Income Statement)

The Profit and Loss Statement will show Christopher his revenue, expenses, and profit.

- **Revenue:** This includes all money earned from mowing lawns and snow removal services.

- **Cost of Goods Sold (COGS):** This includes the cost of fuel for his equipment and any repair costs.
- **Operating Expenses:** These are expenses such as advertising, wages if he hires help, and maintenance of equipment.
- **Net Profit:** This is the amount left after all expenses are deducted from revenue.

By analyzing his Profit and Loss Statement, Christopher can see which services are most profitable, control his costs, and ensure he's making a good profit each season.

Cash Flow Statement

The Cash Flow Statement shows the cash movements in and out of Christopher's business.

- **Operating Activities:** Cash received from customers for services and cash paid for fuel, maintenance, and other operating expenses.
- **Investing Activities:** Cash spent on purchasing new equipment or repairing existing equipment.
- **Financing Activities:** Any loans taken out or repaid.

Monitoring his Cash Flow Statement helps Christopher ensure he has enough cash to cover his expenses, especially during off-peak seasons, and plan for any large upcoming expenditures.

Why It's Important:

For Christopher, keeping track of these financial statements helps him manage the seasonal nature of his business, ensuring he has enough cash flow throughout the year. It allows him to make informed decisions about investments in new equipment, pricing for his services, and controlling costs to maintain profitability.

By understanding and regularly reviewing their Balance Sheet, Profit and Loss Statement, and Cash Flow Statement, both Emmi and Christopher can effectively manage their businesses, make informed decisions, and plan for future growth. These financial statements provide a clear picture of their business's financial health, helping them stay on track and achieve their financial goals.

Summary

Basic Financial Statements and Terms

Understanding these three financial statements - Balance Sheet, Profit and Loss Statement, and Cash Flow Statement - gives you a comprehensive view of a company's financial health. You should at least know what these financial statements are, even if you don't plan on using them every day. Just having a basic understanding can help you make smarter financial decisions, whether it's managing your own budget or running a small business. They're a great way to understand and manage money - both personally and in business. It's all about gaining financial knowledge and building financial awareness.

The Balance Sheet shows what a company (or you) owns and owes at a specific point in time, which is key for making sure you're financially stable. The Profit and Loss Statement reveals how much profit or loss the company made over a period. Personally, it can show whether you're bringing in more money than you're spending, helping you avoid living beyond your means. The Cash Flow Statement tracks the flow of cash in and out of the business or can help you keep track of your cash—so you know if you have enough to cover bills or unexpected expenses. By grasping these concepts, you'll be better equipped to manage your own finances, understand how money flows in your life, and make informed business decisions, whether you choose to take the entrepreneurial leap now or in the future.

CHAPTER 12

HOW THE WORLD PLAYS A ROLE IN YOUR PERSONAL FINANCES

A more complex part of personal finance is understanding how the world we live in - and basic economics - help us make better financial decisions. Understanding how the world around us influences our lives and more importantly, our money, is crucial. Economics isn't just for economists or adults; it affects everyone, including you.

In our daily lives, we constantly interact with economic principles, often without even realizing it. These economic principles help us adjust how we budget our monthly expenses and guide decisions on whether to save or spend. Let's dive into how these principles impact your everyday life and financial decisions.

First, let's clarify some basic economic terms. What is the 'economy.' The economy refers to the entire system of production, distribution, and consumption of goods and services. It operates at multiple levels, including local, national and global. It's essentially a massive marketplace where everything - from cars to coffee beans - is traded. Local examples include farmers' markets where local produce is sold, while global examples involve international trade between countries. In essence, the economy is a dynamic network that connects various players, such as businesses, governments, and consumers. This interconnected system impacts nearly every aspect of our lives, from the prices we pay for goods to the jobs we hold. Understanding how this system works can help you make better financial decisions and understand global events.

The Power of Supply and Demand

In a market economy, prices are set by supply (the availability of something) and demand (how much people want it). If something is in high demand but scarce, prices rise. On the flip side, if there's plenty of something and low demand, prices fall. Businesses then make adjustments to their production based on supply and demand to help balance out shortages and surpluses over time. The government usually stays out of supply and demand, letting businesses make decisions, but sometimes steps in with regulations to ensure fairness and protect consumers.

Let's dive a little deeper into the concept of supply and demand. Let's say you're interested in buying the latest smartphone. If there's high demand for this new phone but the supply is limited, the price will likely be high. On the other hand, if the company produces more phones than people want to buy, the price will drop. Understanding this basic principle helps you decide when to make purchases. So sometimes, waiting a few months after a product release can often save you money as initial demand decreases and more supplies become available. Being aware of these dynamics allows you to time your purchases effectively, ensuring you get the best value for your money even for big ticket items like cars or houses.

Businesses leverage supply and demand information to set prices, plan inventory, and strategize marketing. As a consumer, being informed lets you take advantage of sales and discounts when a product is overstocked.

Ultimately, understanding supply and demand mechanics can not only aid in everyday purchasing decisions but also in larger financial commitments, helping you manage your budget efficiently.

Other Important Economic Terms

Another important term is opportunity cost, which is what you give up when you choose one thing over another. For instance, if you spend your money on a concert ticket, the opportunity cost is what else you could have done with that money. Understanding opportunity cost can have a major impact on your personal financial decisions. Whether you're considering taking out a loan, buying a car, or even choosing between job offers, being aware of what you're giving up will guide you toward the option that is best for you.

Gross Domestic Product (GDP) is a measure of a country's economic performance. It measures the total value of all goods and services produced in a country over a specific period of time, usually a year. It serves as a comprehensive scorecard of a nation's economic health. A growing GDP indicates that a country is producing more goods and services and that usually means a healthy economy with more job opportunities and better living standards. Policymakers and economists closely monitor GDP to gauge the effectiveness of economic policies and make adjustments as needed.

Having a grasp of GDP allows you to understand news reports about the economy better. When you hear that GDP is growing, it usually means businesses are thriving, and job opportunities are rising. On the flip side, a shrinking GDP may signal tough times ahead, encouraging you to save more and spend less.

Economic principles aren't just theories found in textbooks—they have a real and direct impact on our daily lives. For example, economic trends affect how you budget your money. When you create a monthly budget, you're not just deciding what to spend and where; you're influenced by broader economic trends. During good economic times, you might have more income, while during bad times, you might need to save more and spend less.

Inflation is another key concept, referring to the rate at which prices for goods and services rise over time, reducing the purchasing power of your money. When inflation is high, each unit of currency, like the dollar, buys fewer goods and services. This affects everything from groceries to utility bills. For example, if the annual inflation rate is 3%, something that costs $100 this year will cost $103 next year, assuming no other changes. If inflation rates are projected to rise, it might be wise to allocate more of your budget towards savings rather than spending it on wants. When inflation is high, it's wise to allocate more of your budget to savings instead of spending on wants (save more and spend less!). This helps you maintain your purchasing power even as prices for goods and services rise.

During periods of low inflation, you may feel more comfortable making larger purchases or taking on additional debt. Being proactive and strategic about how you handle your finances in response to inflation can help protect your purchasing power over the long term. Recognizing the economy's cyclical nature lets you adjust your financial strategy, whether by cutting non-essential spending or increasing your income.

A critical area influenced by economic principles is the job market. Job market conditions play a pivotal role in determining employment opportunities and wages. When the economy is growing, companies often expand their operations, leading to more job openings and potentially higher wages as the demand for skilled labor increases. On the other hand, during economic recessions, job availability can shrink, and wages may stay the same or even decline.

Understanding job market conditions can guide career choices and professional development. For instance, knowing which industries are flourishing can help you target your job search more effectively or decide on the skills you need to acquire. During times of low unemployment, workers have more leverage to negotiate higher salaries or better benefits. On the other hand, in a high-unemployment scenario, you might need to be flexible regarding job roles and lower your salary expectations.

Job market trends should influence your decisions about further education or training. If a particular industry is projected to grow, getting the relevant education or certification can be a smart move to enhance future employability and wage potential. Conversely, during uncertain economic times, it might be smarter to focus on strengthening and diversifying any existing skills to adapt to shifting job market demands.

Interest rates are an economic principle that play a vital role in daily life, especially when it comes to loans and savings. Interest rates determine both borrowing costs and savings returns, playing a crucial role in everyday life. When interest rates are low, loans become cheaper, encouraging people to take on more debt for things like buying homes, cars, or funding education. Conversely, high-interest rates make borrowing more expensive, which can discourage taking on new loans and encourage more savings. Basically, low interest rates make loans cheaper but offer lower returns on savings, whereas high rates make loans more expensive but offer better returns on savings accounts.

For example, if you secure a mortgage when interest rates are low, you'll pay less over time compared to a high-interest rate period. On the savings side, higher interest rates mean better returns on savings accounts, Certificate of Deposits or fixed-income investments like bonds. Therefore, being aware of current interest rates can inform your decisions about when to borrow, when to save and where to invest.

Understanding how interest rates fluctuate can also help you plan long-term financial goals. Knowing that rates are likely to rise can motivate you to lock in lower rates for any long-term loans you might need. On the other hand, if rates are expected to decline, you might wait to take on new debt to benefit from future lower rates. This insight allows you to optimize your financial strategy according to interest rate cycles, so you get the best possible terms for loans and the highest returns on your savings.

Economic principles also highlight the impact of global events on personal finance. Global events, like trade wars or pandemics, influence local prices and job markets. Staying informed about economic trends through news and financial reports helps you anticipate market changes and adjust your personal finances accordingly.

The Economic Impact of COVID-19

The COVID-19 pandemic has been one of the most significant global events in recent history, not just in terms of health but also in its profound economic implications. As countries around the world implemented lockdowns and social distancing measures, the effects rippled through economies, affecting industries, labor markets, and consumer behavior.

First, we had global supply chain disruptions. As factories in Asia halted production, the ripple effects were felt worldwide. Many industries, such as those in the manufacturing and technology sectors, experienced delays and shortages of key parts and components. This was particularly evident in sectors like electronics and automotive, where inventory dropped due to this sudden disruption.

Restrictions on international travel and trade led to shipping delays and increased costs. Ports experienced congestion as shipping containers piled up, leading to higher prices for goods and contributing to inflation.

There were job losses and an unprecedented increase in the unemployment rates. The hospitality, travel, and retail sectors were hit the hardest. Lockdowns forced businesses to close temporarily or reduce their operations. Millions of workers found themselves furloughed or laid off, leading to skyrocketing unemployment rates in many countries.

While some sectors faced closures, others that could, adapted by shifting to remote work. This shift sped up digital transformation and opened new opportunities in tech and online services.

In response to the economic crisis, governments around the world enacted various stimulus measures to support businesses and individuals. Many countries provided direct financial assistance to citizens, helping to stabilize household incomes and maintain consumer spending during the worst of the pandemic. Governments introduced programs to help struggling businesses with loans, grants, and tax relief. These measures aimed to preserve jobs and keep businesses afloat during the crisis.

The COVID-19 pandemic also led to significant shifts in consumer behavior that may have long-lasting effects. There was a boom in e-commerce. With physical stores closing and consumers staying home, e-commerce experienced explosive growth. Businesses that adapted quickly to online sales thrived, while others struggled to pivot.

As the world begins to emerge from the pandemic, the long-term economic implications are becoming clearer. Many governments and individuals took on significant debt to weather the crisis. Managing this debt in the post-pandemic world will be a major challenge.

Furthermore, governments and businesses alike will need to focus on building resilience to future shocks. This includes investing in technology, diversifying supply chains, and preparing for potential future pandemics.

Summary

How Economic Awareness Shapes Your Future

Understanding how the economy works empowers you to make better financial decisions and be better prepared for the future. Keep learning and staying informed, and you'll be well on your way to managing your finances effectively. How might your newfound understanding of economics change the way you approach your future? Whether it's choosing a career, making investments, or simply deciding how to spend your weekend, these principles will always be at play. So next time you make a financial decision, take a moment to reflect on the local, national and global economic forces at work - you might find yourself making wiser choices.

CHAPTER 13

EMBRACING YOUR MONEY MINDSET AND PREPARING FOR FINANCIAL INDEPENDENCE

As you approach the end of this book, it's time to reflect on everything you've learned and how it will shape your future. One of the key elements of financial success is understanding and mastering your money mindset. Your emotions about money— whether excitement, anxiety, or indifference—have a strong influence on how you manage it. These emotions and thoughts form your "money mindset," which is like your personal financial GPS, guiding you through every financial decision you'll ever make.

The Influence of Your Upbringing on Money Mindset

Take some time to reflect on your childhood and life experiences and how they shaped your view of money. Many people don't realize that their approach to money is deeply rooted in their upbringing and personal experiences. From the time you were a child, you absorbed various ideas about money. Maybe your parents talked about saving every penny, or perhaps you saw friends splurge on things they didn't need. These early experiences influence how you think and feel about money. For example, if your parents frequently worried about bills, you may have inherited some of that anxiety. But if money seemed plentiful in your household, you may have developed a somewhat carefree attitude towards spending. Recognizing these patterns is important because they can either guide you toward financial security or lead to stress and instability.

Identifying Your Money Mindset

Understanding your money mindset helps you make more informed financial decisions. Whether you save every penny, spend impulsively, or fall somewhere in between, gaining insight into your personal money mindset is crucial. Your mindset typically falls into two categories—scarcity and abundance. A scarcity mindset is marked by constant worry that there's never enough, often leading to stress over money. In contrast, an abundance mindset is rooted in the belief that there's always enough, with confidence in your ability to earn and manage it. Identifying which camp you fall into—or if you're somewhere in between—is the first step toward a healthier money mindset.

Setting clear financial goals, both short-term and long-term, can help shift your mindset from scarcity to abundance. By actively working towards something meaningful—whether it's saving for a vacation, paying off student loans, or building an emergency fund—you gain a sense of control over your finances. This sense of purpose reduces financial stress and encourages you to view money as a tool to achieve your dreams, rather than a source of anxiety.

Shifting Your Money Mindset for Better Financial Health

Once you identify your money mindset, it's essential to shift it towards healthier financial habits. Mindfulness is a powerful tool to help you better understand your feelings about money. Being mindful means paying attention to your thoughts and emotions. When you notice yourself stressing about money, take a moment to think about why. Is it because of a real financial issue, or are you reacting based on past experiences? Mindfulness helps you see these patterns more clearly and gives you the power to change them.

Practicing gratitude can also shift your focus from what you lack to what you have. Instead of fixating on not having the latest gadget or the trendiest clothes, try to appreciate what you already own and the financial security you do have. This simple shift can reduce stress and make you feel richer instantly.

Education is another key element. Knowing how to budget, save, and invest wisely empowers you to take control of your financial future. It gives you the tools, and the confidence, to make informed decisions rather than emotional ones. There are plenty of resources out there—books, online courses, and workshops—that can teach you these skills.

Surrounding Yourself with Positive Influences

Your environment and the people in your life have a strong influence on your money mindset. Friends, family, and even online communities can shape your financial habits. Surround yourself with people who have a healthy attitude towards money. Their positive habits can influence you, and you can learn from their experiences. Social media, TV shows, and even your neighborhood all play a part in shaping your money mindset. Be aware of social pressures and avoid falling into the trap of keeping up appearances. Once you recognize these influences, you can decide which ones to keep and which ones to kick to the curb.

In today's social media-driven world, it's easy to fall into the trap of comparing your financial situation to others. Constant exposure to images of luxury lifestyles, shopping hauls, get rich quick schemes and 'success stories' can make you feel like you're behind or not doing enough. It's important to remember that social media often presents a curated, filtered version of reality. Building a healthy money mindset means resisting the urge to compare and instead focusing on your own unique financial journey.

Setting Financial Goals

Breaking down your financial goals into smaller, manageable, and achievable tasks can make them feel less overwhelming. Instead of setting a vague goal like "I want to be rich," try something concrete, like "I will save $500 in the next three months." Smaller goals are easier to achieve and can keep you motivated as you get closer to reaching them and even more motivated to go further once you attain them.

Managing Emotions

Your emotions can have a big impact on your financial decisions. For instance, stress and anxiety might push you to make overly cautious choices, missing out on potentially rewarding opportunities. Of course, overconfidence might lead you to make impulse purchases or make risky decisions without proper planning. Understanding your emotional triggers can help you manage them better, leading to smarter financial choices.

Understanding your thoughts and feelings about money can be a game-changer helping you make better financial decisions. Here are a few activities to help you explore your money mindset:

- List your money habits: Start by jotting down instances where you spend, save, or even avoid thinking about money. Be honest and detailed. Do you tend to splurge on weekends after being frugal all week? Or maybe you stash away every spare dollar, denying yourself small pleasures?
- Reflect on emotions: Next, write down the emotions you feel during these instances. Are you excited when making a purchase, or do you feel guilty afterward? Perhaps saving gives you peace of mind, but also a sense of deprivation?
- Analyze patterns: Look at your lists and try to identify any patterns. Do you spend more when you're feeling down? Or maybe you're super strict with your spending until you get that paycheck, and then it's like a free-for-all?

- Consider influences: Think about how your family, friends, and experiences have shaped your money mindset. Did you grow up in a household where money was tight, leading you to be overly cautious? Or perhaps witnessing a friend's carefree spending has rubbed off on you?

One last, but not least thought, know that everyone makes financial mistakes—whether it's overspending, taking on too much debt, or missing savings goals. But self-compassion is crucial in developing a healthy money mindset. Instead of dwelling on past errors, treat them as learning opportunities. By forgiving yourself and making small, positive changes, you build resilience and can continue to grow financially without letting setbacks define your journey.

Summary

Continuous Improvement and Financial Literacy

Changing your money mindset won't happen overnight. It's not about flipping a switch, but about making continuous, small adjustments. It requires ongoing effort and self-reflection. Continuously work on understanding and improving your emotional responses to money. The more you understand your relationship with money, the better decisions you will make, leading to a happier and more financially secure life. Your mindset is one of the most powerful tools for achieving financial wellness.

Reflect on everything you've learned and how it will shape your future. Each positive step you take builds the foundation for a more secure financial future. Understanding your unique money mindset is a powerful first step. Being mindful of your emotional triggers can keep you from making rash decisions that could harm your financial future. It's essential to be aware of the influence of social pressures, too. Chasing trends or trying to keep up with others can lead to unnecessary debt and financial strain.

Each positive step you take builds the foundation for a more secure financial future. Reflect on what you've learned here. Your journey towards financial wellness begins with the choices you make today. You have the power to shape your financial story.

CONCLUSION

EMPOWERING YOUNG ADULTS FOR FINANCIAL SUCCESS

This book was designed with one goal: to help you make informed financial decisions with confidence. By reflecting on what you've learned and applying it to real-life situations, you can set yourself up for future success and yes, financial independence. This journey towards financial empowerment can be both exciting and incredibly rewarding.

Many young adults today find themselves unprepared for financial independence. They might know the basics, like saving money or perhaps managing a part-time job salary, but the bigger picture can seem blurry. Like budgeting—it's one thing to create a budget but sticking to it is another challenge altogether. Or take investing: many find it intimidating to explore stock markets or understand mutual funds. Avoiding debt and maintaining good credit are often overlooked until it's too late. These are common hurdles that young people face, underscoring the need for practical advice and resources tailored to your unique situation.

Hopefully you found valuable insights and tools in this book to help bridge these gaps in your financial knowledge. We've walked you through learning about essential topics, helped you identify areas where you can improve and how to create a personalized financial plan. You've also learned about leveraging modern tools and technologies like apps that make managing money easier. Essentially, we aimed to empower you with practical strategies and relatable examples, ensuring that you're well-equipped to achieve financial security. Whether you're already savvy with money or just starting to pay attention to your finances, this book's main goal was to enhance your understanding and boost your confidence in handling money matters.

Reflecting on what you've learned so far is an essential step in preparing for a financially secure future. You've covered a lot of ground through the chapters, and taking a moment to consolidate that knowledge can make all the difference. Remember, financial literacy is about having the information and also understanding how to apply it to your unique situation.

Think back to many times we've referenced budgeting, saving, investing, managing credit, and avoiding debt. Each of these topics has provided you with valuable tools and insights that can transform how you handle money. Crafting a budget might have felt challenging at first, but over time, you likely saw how creating a structured plan for your income made managing your expenses more straightforward. Reflect on those early experiences and consider how much easier budgeting has become over time.

Your progress in financial literacy is significant. Hopefully, you've noticed changes in your spending habits or are ready to take action to make necessary adjustments. Perhaps now you're more cautious about unnecessary purchases or more proactive in setting aside savings each month. These small but meaningful changes are signs of growth and should be celebrated. At the same time, it's crucial to identify areas where you can still improve. Maybe you're great at saving but find investing intimidating, or perhaps you struggle to keep track of your daily expenses. Acknowledging these areas gives you a clear idea of where to focus next.

Continuous learning is at the heart of financial security. As you move forward, consider maintaining a journal where you can jot down financial milestones, challenges, and goals. Not only does this practice help you keep track of your journey, but it also serves as a reflective tool to see how far you've come. Imagine looking back a year from now and seeing the positive changes in your financial behaviors and attitudes, and yes, even your balances in your accounts!

Here is what you can do to organize your thoughts and start your financial journal:

- Start by defining your short-term and long-term financial goals.
- Next, outline your current financial status by listing your assets, liabilities, income, and expenses.
- Develop strategies to achieve your goals, such as increasing savings, reducing unnecessary expenses, or seeking investment opportunities.

Having a personalized financial plan keeps you focused and motivated as you work towards your goals. Moreover, reflection plays a critical role in solidifying your learning. Taking time to think deeply about your financial decisions and their outcomes helps reinforce good habits and correct mistakes. Set aside a few minutes each week to assess your spending, saving, and investing behaviors. This regular reflection will not only help you stay on track but will also instill a greater sense of discipline and accountability.

Financial literacy is a lifelong journey. Even as you gain more knowledge and experience, there will always be new challenges and opportunities to learn. Stay curious and open-minded, and don't hesitate to seek out additional knowledge or even professional advice when needed. Engaging with credible sources and continuously educating yourself ensures that you remain informed and capable of making sound financial decisions.

Stay updated on new financial trends and technologies that could benefit you. Whether it's exploring digital banking tools, learning about emerging investment opportunities, or understanding changes in tax legislation, keeping up to date with these developments equips you with the knowledge to navigate the future financial landscape effectively.

Integrating financial education into your daily life can be as simple as discussing money management topics with friends or family. Sharing experiences and strategies can provide new insights and strengthen your financial awareness. You might find that others have encountered similar challenges and can offer valuable advice or perspective. Creating a supportive network fosters an environment where financial literacy becomes a shared goal, encouraging continuous improvement.

If you know someone who owns their own business, ask them to go over their Profit and Loss with you. Talk to an adult in your life about what they are investing in or how they're saving for retirement. Ask your parents to go over their tax return with you. Sometimes, sharing experiences and strategies can offer valuable advice and fresh perspectives. Plus, it creates a supportive network where everyone is working towards financial literacy together.

Finally, don't underestimate the value of professional help. Financial advisors, counselors, and educators are invaluable resources for personalized guidance and support. Don't be afraid to ask questions or seek advice tailored to your specific needs and circumstances. Educating yourself about personal finance and investing is crucial for making informed decisions about your money. Sometimes, an expert opinion can provide clarity and direction that self-study alone cannot.

In conclusion, reflecting on your financial literacy journey is a powerful step towards securing your future. By reviewing key concepts periodically, assessing your progress, and identifying areas for improvement, you create a foundation for continual growth. Embrace tools like journaling and personal financial planning, engage in continuous learning, and seek support from credible resources, friends and family and professionals.

Remember, financial literacy is a long journey—one where every step forward brings you closer to financial empowerment and stability. Keep learning, stay curious, and you can easily take control of your financial future. Your journey is just beginning, and with the right knowledge, desire to learn more and the right mindset, you're well-equipped to succeed.

Final Thoughts from the Authors

We've equipped you with the tools to step confidently into adulthood, ready to make wise financial decisions that will benefit you throughout your lives. Now that you possess this knowledge, you are miles ahead of many of your peers in terms of money management. But your journey doesn't end here—there's an opportunity for you to take on a new role: an advocate for financial literacy.

Your understanding of budgeting, credit, loans, taxes, and investments puts you in a unique position to share what you've learned. By spreading the word about the importance of financial literacy to your friends, family, and even school administrators, you can contribute to closing the financial knowledge gap that exists in so many communities.

Think about it: schools require courses in subject matters like math, science, history, physical education and arts, yet many neglect financial literacy, a life skill essential for everyday survival. While learning about cloud formations or historical figures is important, those lessons don't often have an immediate impact on your financial stability. Yet understanding how to manage money, avoid debt, and make informed investments has a direct influence on your future.

Consider the example of students in Ohio who participated in a state-mandated financial literacy course. They didn't just learn about budgeting—they were also taught about credit, taxes, loans, and insurance – all of the topics we've covered in this book. The results were compelling: those students had higher credit scores and lower default rates compared to their peers in states where financial literacy wasn't mandated. These outcomes underscore the significant difference financial education can make in young adults' lives.

The fact that financial literacy isn't a nationwide requirement in schools is alarming. Too many students graduate without the foundational knowledge they need to navigate financial challenges. That's why we believe there needs to be a shift toward integrating financial education in schools across the country, ensuring that every young person leaves school prepared to manage their finances wisely.

The time has come for us to advocate for change. And you can be a part of this change!

You can take action to address this gap. Spread the knowledge you've acquired by telling your friends and family about this book. Encourage them to learn about financial literacy alongside you. You can also make an impact by advocating for financial education in your school. Talk to your school administrators about the importance of including financial literacy in the curriculum—whether through a dedicated semester course or assemblies that feature engaging guest speakers, like us!

We're passionate about helping young adults gain the skills they need to succeed. We love it when we partner with schools to create a comprehensive financial literacy program or host assemblies that bring financial concepts to life through interactive presentations and Q&A sessions. We have already inspired many students to take control of their financial futures and we hope, after reading this book, you too are now one of them.

Your efforts can also cause a ripple effect. When you speak up, you help create awareness about the need for financial education. Your advocacy can lead to real change, not only in your school but also in your community. By encouraging your peers to embrace financial literacy, you help build a future where more young adults are equipped to handle their finances responsibly.

Remember, your voice matters. Whether you're sharing what you've learned, advocating for change in your school, or taking steps to further your own financial education, you're making a difference. You have the power to inspire others, and through collective action, we can create a generation, and future generations, that are not only financially literate but also financially empowered.

Join us on this journey toward financial independence for all. Keep learning, keep advocating, and keep inspiring others to do the same. Together, we can build a future where financial literacy is a priority for everyone.

Connect with us on our social media platforms.

www.dollarsandsensepublishing.com

dollarsandsensepub@gmail.com

BONUS FINANCIAL SUCCESS STARTER PACK!

Step 1) Scan the code below to be directed to an exclusive website

Step 2) Enter your email address for your bonus materials

Step 3) Do nothing – we'll deliver the Dollars and Sense Financial Success Starter Pack directly to your inbox within 24 hours.

It's packed with actionable tips, strategies and visuals that make financial literacy even easier to understand and master!

THANK YOU FOR READING!

We hope you've enjoyed reading this book and, more importantly, that it has equipped you with the tools and knowledge to make confident, informed financial decisions. It's been an honor to accompany you on your journey toward financial literacy.

If this book has been helpful, we would love for you to leave a review on Amazon. Your feedback not only supports us but also helps others decide if this book could be a valuable resource for their own financial journey.

Your feedback can help spread the importance of financial literacy and inspire others to take control of their financial futures.

REFERENCES

1st United Credit Union. (n.d.). Start building or improving your credit with our tips.

https://www.1stunitedcu.org/more-for-you/financial-wellness/five-best-ways-to-build-credit

A Stepping Stone Foundation. (2023). Scholarship success story - The story of Rosa!. A Stepping Stone Foundation.

https://asteppingstone.org/blog/scholarship-story-of-rosa/

Ackman, A. (2021). Needs Vs. Wants: How to Tell the Difference.

https://www.forritcu.org/needs-vs-wants-how-to-tell-the-difference/

Annuity.org. (2024). How to Manage Your Money & Be Financially Successful.

https://www.annuity.org/financial-literacy/

Arpaci, I., Aslan, O., & Kevser, M. (2024). Evaluating short- and long-term investment strategies: development and validation of the investment strategies scale (ISS). Financial Innovation

https://doi.org/10.1186/s40854-023-00573-4

ATFCU. Why is financial literacy important for students.

https://www.atfcu.org/about/telco-blog/why-is-financial-literacy-important-for- students

Battered Women's Support Services. (n.d.). Budgeting, saving, investments & education - BWSS. [Webpage].

https://www.bwss.org/resources/economic-empowerment-strategies-for-women/budgeting-saving-investment-and-education/

Bloomsburg University Foundation. (n.d.). Scholarships can change the course of students' lives and make their dreams a reality.

https://giving.bloomu.edu/your-impact/stories-of-impact-support.

Bogleheads Forum

https://www.bogleheads.org/forum/viewtopic.php?t=349426

Business LibreTexts. (2023). Taxes and Financial Planning. Business LibreTexts.

https://biz.libretexts.org/Bookshelves/Finance/Individual_Finance/06%3A_Taxes_and_Tax_Planning/6.04%3A_Taxes_and_Financial_Planning

Calculators.org. (n.d.). Overtime Pay Calculator.

https://www.calculators.org/savings/overtime.php.

CashCourse. (n.d.). Is it a Need or a Want? Here's How to Tell.

https://www.cashcourse.org/Topics/Spend/Spending-Decisions/Is-it-a-Need-or-a-Want-Heres-How-to-Tell

Center for Financial Literacy. (2017). 2017 Case Summary.

https://financialliteracy.champlain.edu/research-advocacy/2017-national-report-card-on-high-school-financial-literacy/2017-case-summary/

Center for Social Development. (2017). Can America compete?

https://www.nefe.org/news/nefe-digest/2017/can-america-compete

Champlain College. (2017). 2017 Case Summary - Center for Financial Literacy. Champlain College.

https://financialliteracy.champlain.edu/research-advocacy/2017-national-report-card-on-high-school-financial-literacy/2017-case-summary/

CIAAGO.

http://www.ciaago.org/index-1367.html

Cobo, S. (2021). 5 Financial Habits That Can Improve Your Credit Score. Quorum.

https://www.quorumfcu.org/learn/money-management/5-financial-habits-that-can-improve-your-credit-score/

Cobo, S. (2019). Five strategies to help shrink credit card debt. Quorum.

https://www.quorumfcu.org/learn/money-management/five-strategies-to-help-shrink-credit-card-debt/

Consolidated Credit. (n.d.). Teenagers & Credit Cards.

https://www.consolidatedcredit.org/family-finances/teens-and-credit-cards/

Consumer Financial Protection Bureau. (n.d.). An essential guide to building an emergency fund.

https://www.consumerfinance.gov/an-essential-guide-to-building-an-emergency- fund/

Consumer Financial Protection Bureau. (n.d.). How do I get and keep a good credit score?

https://www.consumerfinance.gov/ask-cfpb/how-do-i-get-and-keep-a-good-credit-score-en-318/

Consumer Financial Protection Bureau. (n.d.). How does compound interest work?

https://www.consumerfinance.gov/ask-cfpb/how-does-compound-interest-work-en-1683/

Consumer Financial Protection Bureau. (n.d.). Learn more: Navigating financial regulations

https://www.consumerfinance.gov/learnmore

Consumer Reports. (2021). How to Be a Smarter Shopper Right Now. Money.

https://www.consumerreports.org/shopping/how-to-be-a-smarter-shopper-right-now/

Credit Counselling Society. (2023). 12 Tips to Use a Credit Card but Not End Up in Debt

https://nomoredebts.org/credit/how-to-use-credit-card

CSMD, Financial Literacy and Budgeting. (n.d.). Financial Literacy and Budgeting.

https://www.csmd.edu/costs-aid/financial-literacy/index.html

DC Fiscal Policy Institute. (2022). Money Matters: Adequate and Targeted Investments in Education Can Help Reduce Opportunity Gaps. DC Fiscal Policy Institute.

https://www.dcfpi.org/all/money-matters/

Debt.org. (2023). 14 Easy Ways to Cut Expenses at Home.

https://www.debt.org/advice/how-to-cut-expenses/

Debt.org. (2023). Using a credit card to build credit.

https://www.debt.org/credit/report/build-credit-with-credit-card/

Díaz, A., Esparcia, C., & López, R. (2022). The diversifying role of socially responsible investments during the COVID-19 crisis: A risk management and portfolio performance analysis. Economic Analysis and Policy, 75(39).

https://doi.org/10.1016/j.eap.2022.05.001

Drexel University. (n.d.). Grants, Scholarships & Loans: What's the Difference?.

https://drexel.edu/soe/admissions/financial-aid/difference-between-student-grants-vs-loans/

Duke K McAdow. (2020). Best practices and expectations. Finance & Business.

https://financeandbusiness.ucdavis.edu/bia/budget/budget-framework/best-practices

EECU. (n.d.). Online scams targeting teens and young adults. EECU.

https://eecu.org/community/articles/online-scams-targeting-teens-and-young-adults

Evening Optimist Club of Sumter. (n.d.). Investing for beginners.

http://eveningoptimistclubofsumter.org/investing-for-beginners.html

Fairwinds. (n.d.). How to Tell the Difference Between Your Wants and Needs.

https://www.fairwinds.org/articles/how-to-tell-the-difference-between-your-wants-and-needs

FHI 360. (2022). Budgeting for needs and wants.

https://www.fhi360.org/resources/budgeting-needs-and-wants/

Forbes, N. (2022). A Realist's Guide to Investing for Good. Stanford Social Innovation Review.

https://ssir.org/articles/entry/a_realists_guide_to_investing_for_good

Glendale Community College. (n.d.). Insurance/Risk Management.

https://www.glendale.edu/students/student-services/career-center/recommended-web-resources/researching-careers-majors/career-profiles/insurance-risk-management

Great Lakes Credit Union. (n.d.). Investing for Kids and Teens.

https://www.glcu.org/blog/blog-details/?news_cat=money-smarts&news_article=investing-for-kids-and-teens

Ham, H. (2021). 2 Ways to Bring Games Into Your Classroom. Edutopia.

https://www.edutopia.org/article/two-ways-bring-games-your-classroom/

Harvard Business Review. (2010). When you've got to cut costs—now.

https://hbr.org/2010/05/when-youve-got-to-cut-costs-now

Harvard Business Review. Making Smart Investments: A Beginner's Guide.

https://hbr.org/2021/08/how-to-make-smart-investments-a-beginners-guide

Hirsch, P. (2023). The case for financial literacy education. Planet Money.

https://www.npr.org/sections/money/2023/05/16/1176189034/the-case-for-financial-literacy-education

Huddleston Jr., T. (2023). Mark Cuban: 'People thought I was an idiot' for launching the company I sold for billions. CNBC.com

https://www.cnbc.com/2023/01/15/mark-cuban-on-broadcastcom-streaming-people-thought-i-was-an-idiot.html

InCharge Debt Solutions. (2024). 7 Reasons You Should Make a Budget: The Benefits of Budgeting.

https://www.incharge.org/financial-literacy/budgeting-saving/budgeting-benefits/

Insurance Information Institute. (2017). Risk management basics.

https://www.iii.org/publications/insuring-your-business-small-business-owners-guide-to-insurance/risk-management/risk-management-basics

Internal Revenue Service. (2023). Tax credits for individuals: What they mean and how they can help refunds. IRS Fact Sheet.

https://www.irs.gov/newsroom/tax-credits-for-individuals-what-they-mean-and-how-they-can-help-refunds

Internet Matters. (2023). Common online scams targeting teens.

https://www.internetmatters.org/hub/expert-opinion/common-online-scams-targeting-teenagers/

ISTE. (n.d.). 5 ways to gamify your classroom.

https://iste.org/blog/5-ways-to-gamify-your-classroom

Knisley, M. (2023). 6 Strategies to Pay Off $20,000 in Credit Card Debt. InCharge Debt Solutions.

https://www.incharge.org/debt-relief/debt-management/how-to-pay-off-20000-credit-card-debt/

Mangis, L. (2019). 12 Ways To Shop Smarter This Year. Advantage CCS.

https://www.advantageccs.org/blog/12-ways-to-shop-smarter-this-year-2/

Mangis, L. (2018). Should Your Teenager Have A Credit Card? Advantage CCS.

https://www.advantageccs.org/blog/should-your-teenager-have-a-credit-card/

Marquette University. (n.d.). Scholarship Impact Stories.

https://give.marquette.edu/scholarship-impact-stories

Marymount University. (2021, October 5). 14 tips for completing fantastic scholarship applications. Marymount University.

https://marymount.edu/blog/14-tips-for-completing-fantastic-scholarship-applications/

Members1stFederalCreditUnion. (n.d.). How to Teach Teens About Budgeting Their Money

https://www.members1st.org/blog/articles/teach-teens-about-budgeting/

Morris, G. (2024). How To Cut Your Expenses. InCharge Debt Solutions.

https://www.incharge.org/financial-literacy/budgeting-saving/how-to-cut-your-expenses/

Narayan, S. W., Rehman, M. U., Ren, Y.-S., Ma, C. (2023). Is a correlation-based investment strategy beneficial for long-term international portfolio investors?

https://doi.org/10.1186/s40854-023-00471-9

NASAA. (n.d.). Compound Interest - NASAA.

https://www.nasaa.org/investor-education/millennial-money-mission/compound-interest-2/

NEFE. (n.d.). Young adults. Toolkit: Evaluation Perspectives.

https://toolkit.nefe.org/evaluation-resources/evaluation-perspectives/financial-education-groups/young-adults

NGPF. (n.d.). The Power of Starting Early: Why Young People Should Invest When They're Ready.

https://www.ngpf.org/blog/investing/the-power-of-starting-early-why-young-people-should-invest-when-theyre-ready/

NTLCC. (n.d.). Financial Aid Tips for Students.

https://www.nltcc.edu/about/blog/1632841/financial-aid-tips-for-students

Penn Student Registration & Financial Services. (n.d.). Popular Budgeting Strategies.

https://srfs.upenn.edu/financial-wellness/browse-topics/budgeting/popular-budgeting-strategies

Penn Student Registration & Financial Services. (n.d.). The Power of Compound Interest.

https://srfs.upenn.edu/financial-wellness/blog/power-compound-interest

QuickBooks. (n.d.). Payroll expenses: A small business guide for 2023.

http://www.ciaago.org/index-1210.html

Rivermark Credit Union. (n.d.). 7 easy steps to build an emergency fund.

https://www.rivermarkcu.org/blog/savings-strategies/7-easy-steps-to-build-an-emergency-fund/

Stanford Institute for Economic Policy Research (SIEPR). How Do Tax Policies Affect Individuals and Businesses?

https://siepr.stanford.edu/publications/policy-brief/how-do-tax-policies-affect-individuals-and-businesses

Take Charge America. (2022). Understanding the Difference Between Wants and Needs.

https://www.takechargeamerica.org/understanding-wants-vs-needs/

Tax Policy Center. What are tax credits and how do they differ from tax deductions?

https://www.taxpolicycenter.org/briefing-book/what-are-tax-credits-and-how-do-they-differ-tax-deductions

Team SESLOC. (2024). Tips for Improving & Maintaining a Healthy Credit Score. SESLOC Credit Union.

https://www.sesloc.org/tips-for-improving-maintaining-a-healthy-credit-score/

Texas Department of Insurance. (n.d.). How to shop for low cost health insurance

https://www.tdi.texas.gov/consumer/health-insurance-shopping-guide.html

Trailhead Credit Union. (2024). 4 Strategies for Building an Emergency Fund.

https://www.trailheadcu.org/4-strategies-for-building-an-emergency-fund/

UC Berkeley Financial Aid & Scholarships. (2024). Creating a spending plan.

https://financialaid.berkeley.edu/financial-literacy-and-resources/creating-a-spending-plan/

UMass Global. (n.d.). 12 Top Financial Aid Tips and Tricks for College Students.

https://www.umassglobal.edu/news-and-events/blog/top-financial-aid-tips-and-tricks

University of Oregon. (n.d.). Scholarship tips.

https://financialaid.uoregon.edu/scholarships_tips

University of Pennsylvania. (n.d.). Popular budgeting strategies.

https://srfs.upenn.edu/financial-wellness/browse-topics/budgeting/popular-budgeting-strategies

US Career Institute. (n.d.). A High Schooler's Guide to Budgeting.

https://www.uscareerinstitute.edu/blog/high-schoolers-guide-to-budgeting

U.S. Department of Education. Studentaid.gov. Grants.

https://studentaid.gov/understand-aid/types/grants

U.S. Department of Education. Studentaid.gov. Scholarships.

https://studentaid.gov/understand-aid/types/scholarships

U.S. Department of Education. Studentaid.gov. Scholarship tips.

https://studentaid.gov/articles/scholarship-tips/

U.S. Department of Education. Studentaid.gov. Types of Aid.

https://studentaid.gov/understand-aid/types

Weisbaum, H. (2023). Seven top strategies for being a smart consumer. Consumers' Checkbook.

https://www.checkbook.org/san-francisco-bay-area/consumers-notebook/articles/Seven-Top-

Strategies-for-Being-a-Smart-Consumer-7749

WWFCU. (2018). Building Credit: Teens and Credit Cards. Wayne Westland Federal Credit Union.

https://wwfcu.org/media/blog/building-credit-teens-and-credit-cards/

Yale University. (n.d.). Budgeting and goal setting.

https://finlit.yale.edu/planning/budgeting-and-goal-setting